Daring to Feel

Awaken the Healer Within

Alison Lingwood

Feelhealshare Publishing

ISBN 978-1-7398762-0-3

Front cover image Russell Burden.
Front cover design and internal book layout Suzanne Swan.
Printed in United Kingdom.

Disclaimer and Reader Agreement

Although due diligence has been used in researching and authenticating the information contained in this book, the author makes no representations as to accuracy, completeness, currency, suitability, or validity of any opinions expressed in this book. By reading this book, you, the reader, consent to bear sole responsibility for your own decisions to read or use any of this book's material. The information in this book is shared to support you on your journey to improved health and wellbeing and in no way does it constitute medical or mental health advice. The applications in this book are not to be used as a substitute for medical treatments and if you feel the need for medical help, you are advised to consult with your physician and/or mental health provider. The author shall not be liable for any damages or costs of any type arising out of any action taken by you or others based upon reliance on any materials in this book. However, it is the author's sincere prayer that this book be truly helpful to you.

Visit www.feelhealshare.com

I dedicate this book to all those who choose to cultivate joy and positive energy in their lives and to the miracle of the ever-present healing potential of the human being.

Hidden Within

The Creator gathered all of creation and said, "I want to hide something from the humans until they are ready for it. It is the realization that they create their own reality."
The Eagle said, "Give it to me. I will take it to the moon."
The Creator said, "No. One day they will go there and find it."
The Salmon said, "I will bury it on the bottom of the ocean."
The Creator said, "No. They will go there too."
The Buffalo said, "I will bury it on the Great Plains."
The Creator said, "They will cut into the skin of the earth and find it even there."
Grandmother Mole, who lives in the breast of Mother Earth, and who has no physical eyes, but sees with spiritual eyes, said, "Put it inside of them."
And the Creator said, "It is done."

— A Hopi Creation Story

CONTENTS

Introduction

I was sobbing at my daughter's bedside. She had just received two blood transfusions, and the pediatrician had told me that she was suffering from the chronic inflammatory bowel disease, ulcerative colitis. She would have to be on medication for the rest of her life. I was devastated, but as a stubborn seeker of truth, I was not going to blindly accept one doctor's stark diagnosis and treatment plan. A heated discussion ensued—with the doctor offering a dismissive challenge: that I should come back if I found another way. His last throwaway comment was meant to discourage me from wasting my time with "any alternative methods" of treatment. He wrote to my general practitioner stating I was not taking my daughter's illness seriously. I'm sure he believed he was right, but I am also sure he had no idea of the power and determination of the mother, health researcher, and physiotherapist standing in front of him. The fire in my belly was lit.

Some time later, I realized that what upset me the most was being told there was only one way to deal with my daughter's colitis. For almost a year my daughter faithfully took the medications he'd prescribed. Her condition went up and down but there was no clear evidence of healing, and the approach became increasingly frustrating and exhausting for both of us.

The Power of Self-Healing

The universe is constantly challenging us to follow our truth. Nine months after my daughter's diagnosis while our family was on holiday in Italy, she had a severe bowel episode with bleeding and diarrhea. Her condition required immediate treatment, but we hadn't brought the steroids the pediatrician had recommended for emergencies. As a physiotherapist, I had been developing my own healing methods for more than a decade at that point, drawing on the expertise of Richard Flook[1], Dr. Alex Lloyd[2], and many others. But I hadn't had the confidence to intervene in my own daughter's healing. As I struggled with the realization of my limited options, I knew that if ever my beloved daughter needed her mother's loving, healing energy, this was the time. Guiding her with my voice and breath, I centered myself and drew on all of my beliefs in the healing therapies I had learned.

With the help of Dr. Lloyd's empowering method and the persistence of a mother's love, my daughter's symptoms abated in just four days. We continued with this alternative to prescription medication for another five days, at which time she began doing the process herself, reconnecting with her creative essence and allowing her own body's innate healing wisdom to take over. Later, she told me she would have been afraid to tell the pediatrician that she had gone against his recommendation. But the truth was clear: she could feel herself getting better. This was a pivotal confidence-boosting moment for us both.

Since then, despite academic pressures, a parental divorce, moving away from home and numerous other stressors, she has experienced minimal symptoms and hasn't taken any of the medicine. We are both, of course, ever respectful of the wonderful emergency treatment she received initially, and at the same time, her journey has shown us the importance of remaining open to new ways of healing.

---

[1] Richard Flook, *Why Am I Sick?* (London: Hay House UK, 2013).

[2] Alexander Loyd and Ben Johnson, *The Healing Code: 6 Minutes to Heal the Source of Your Health, Success, or Relationship Issue* (New York: Grand Central Publishing, 2012).

This experience with my daughter and similar experiences with many patients over the last 35 years gave me the deep resolve to share some of the techniques I have used and some of the remarkable stories of healing I have witnessed.

> *"Magic is believing in yourself. If you can do that, you can make anything happen."*
>
> – Johann Wolfgang von Goethe

As children, we have an innate trust in the possibility of being and doing whatever our hearts desire. We see life as an adventure, a continuous play of discovery and experience, moving fluidly, playing, and changing identities many times a day. We're infused with the spark of life, creating and reinventing: being a princess one minute, a policeman or fireman the next, playing doctor, or building a fort. As children, our reality is ever-changing. We don't have fixed ideas and move seamlessly from one event and epoch to another, embracing whatever we encounter. We have preferences about our choice of play, which can lead to conflicts with friends, but these silly scraps are soon forgotten.

Children don't recognize the constraints of time and space, which can be a huge advantage. Within the formless space of their imagination children can create complex realities with greater ease than most adults. Children often have a direct sense of what's needed within themselves and are content to listen to their intelligent internal feedback systems. They create their own stories about the world, voice their ideas, then let them go and move on to a different game.

Children help us 're-member' this stream of fluid energy that is our body. 'Re-membering' is to bring back into wholeness all that we are, connecting to our original source and to our natural environment. Ancient wisdom says that our bones represent the rocks of the earth and all the wisdom and structure that has been present for millennia. Perhaps it is the arrangement of the mineral crystals in our bodies that resonate our personal story? When we widen our awareness, we receive direct information, ideas, and inspiration. We may have experienced this holding an infant in our arms and feeling our problems dissolve as we once again *realize* this boundless consciousness. In this same way, we can address our pain with imagination and free-flowing creativity, nurturing this natural course of regeneration.

As we leave childhood, most of us lose our connection with this playground and forget our dreams; we mistrust the guiding light that once shone in us so brightly. We lose the sense of fluid reality, that continuum of existence, and replace it with fixed thought patterns. We separate from the wholeness of our nature to please caregivers and become less able or unable to experience and express fully our limitless, intuitive connections with the invisible world. And this partition grows higher with each passing year.

I still remember a time before losing these connections—how I felt I could swim underwater and breathe like a dolphin; talk with clouds; how seedlings would giggle and grow with delight under the warmth of sun; how my grazed knee was already mending as my mother rubbed the smelly ointment on it. The beauty in these connections was utterly real. I think we all, at one time or another, believed the world worked exactly like this.

"In every real man, a child is hidden that wants to play."

– Friedrich Nietzsche

Sadly, in our adult lives these beliefs and experiences may appear far removed, distant from our current perceptions of the universe. Our pain and suffering become trapped as in the game of hide and seek; we hide from feelings and sensations to avoid fear and feelings of overwhelm or perhaps from hearing the intractable words of a diagnosis. But when we're able to embrace our sensations and emotions as they are, openings may appear, insights may arise, and the physical pain can release.

I have written this book to share my experiences and offer ideas that may allow you to change the ways you think, feel, and experience pain. Every aspect of our design encourages a unique, creative exploration along the path to wholeness; calling us to integrate our painful separated parts into pain-free wellness. The body speaks to us to make us aware of areas that lack integration, and as we *listen*, we can reconnect these fragments at our own pace.

I invite you to explore the mysterious yet beautiful potential for regeneration that is within each of us, so you can once again experience your essential loving nature, creativity, and the unity that surrounds it all. I offer knowledge and guidance in the form of daily tools and practices you can use to help you navigate life's encounters, as well as case studies and personal stories of healings for your reflection.

The body is the vehicle through which we process and share our experience of the world. The tools in this book are offered to help you develop a more authentic, intimate connection with yourself and others. Each of us can learn to be less reactive and more responsive and to navigate all that we encounter with greater ease and wisdom. I call these tools Concentra, a sensing and spatial orientation process that can alleviate chronic pain and the symptoms of illness. This process helps us develop intuition, insights, and instincts and, as our conscious awareness expands, we learn to hear our inner voice more often and more clearly. Concentra can help settle emotions and bring peace and clarity to any situation. Once these new connections are established, we are opened to the freedom of a richer and more meaningful experience of life.

Using breath, Concentra gently uncovers and helps dissolve the stuckness that has prevented our bodies and minds from fully healing. Through the experience of our physical sensations, visualizations, and feelings, we can access a different awareness. By embracing these spontaneous sensory gifts with curiosity, love, compassion, joy, and kindness, we may discover new bonds of healing and a return to wholeness. This simple exchange of energy can transform past injury and illness and allow us to live again more harmoniously with ourselves and others. There is no drama or need to discuss the problem in detail, for rather than consciously letting go of anything, these changes happen in the moment as we engage with a different energetic space.

Organization of the Book

This book is a guide to help you unveil different aspects of yourself and integrate these "parts" so that you may recognize the gifts and talents that greater wholeness brings. It's an invitation to think differently, to approach life with new and greater awareness. Such a realization is wondrous and empowering, as you discover that you play an essential part in creating and healing the universe around you.

From the beauty of nature we can draw to us inspiration by recognizing that the elements are within us, that there are many energies weaving through our space that can help us explore our own personal journey. We can truly create transformations in our health and in our life. The buried treasure lies within us, but like the lotus growing from the mud, we struggle within ourselves before emerging as beautiful flowers.

Although I am British I have chosen to use the American English spelling in this book to reach a broader audience.

The first part of the book is about my journey within the healing arts. It explores my work as a physiotherapist and my growing frustration with how pain is managed in most of the healthcare profession. As this frustration propelled me to search for alternatives, I began to realize even more the importance of the therapist's presence in the patient's healing.

The second part of the book explores pain and our perception of pain. We will look at how our bodies are at one with the world—both as a reflection and a focused source of light. This will enable us to see ourselves more clearly and share our light and presence with others. We will learn that there are far more factors at play concerning pain in our bodies than our nervous system and pain receptors. As we integrate all of the communication systems within our bodies, we will see that we already have regenerative and receptive tools at our service with which to co-create optimal health.

The third part of the book explores, instinct, faith, and our connections with the world around us. We learn to deepen our relationship with nature and the cosmos and remember how the curiosity of our inner child enchants the world into being.

The fourth section offers practical breathing and meditation techniques and the Concentra healing process. By opening to our subtle energies and the five elements of nature, you will become more aligned and balanced, more able to feel, heal, and share intimately with yourself and others.

I invite you to play with and personalize this process for your own needs. Other ideas, insights, techniques, and therapies can be integrated with it too. Open to your spirit's "artistic freedom." There is never just one right way. Discover what works best for you.

At the end of some of the chapters there are "Thoughts of Germination," reminders of the essence of each narrative.

"If you want the truth, I'll tell you the truth.
Listen to the secret sound, the real sound which is inside you."

– Kabir

Part 1

My Journey to Concentra

Chapter 1

Attuning to Healing

"You have good hands," my A-Level biology teacher observed. "I think you should be a doctor." I have to admit that dissecting the worm and then the rat's intestines did seem to be going well, and so in that moment I pictured myself a surgeon in a prestigious white coat. Not long after, I ditched French to study physics, but even as I began to plan a career in medicine, I knew I didn't want to become a regular doctor.

That sensibility didn't change. As I saw the men in white coats walking up the steps of the London Hospital in Whitechapel, I knew the surgeon's path was not my calling. So I chose to be a physiotherapist—that felt true for me—and it was then that my love affair with the human body began in earnest. As time went on and I became more attuned to the benefits of holistic healing, I was thankful for my choice. For more than 35 years, I have witnessed magical transformations of patients who came to me with all kinds of pains and disabilities. I have been able to apply creativity and flexibility in my choices of therapies, which upon reflection was key to their return to wellness.

During my physiotherapy studies and ever since, I've continued to discover the unique relationships and connections the human body creates within itself and with the outside world. For example, I was initially taught that restricted and painful movement in a lower cervical vertebra indicated that there was a problem with a disc, and if there was also arm pain, a trapped nerve. Logical and confined. What could be easier? I would give the recommended treatment and advice, but sometimes it didn't work. This led me to wonder, what other connections were playing a part in the maintenance of the pain?

Over the years, I've discovered that this "one-size-fits-all" formula works sometimes but not always, and I became increasingly frustrated each time I was unable to relieve a patient's pain. I became cross with myself and even with them. *Why aren't you getting better?* I attended countless classes, spent lots of money, sought out the best teachers, studied in England and overseas, and still felt sad and defeated. I followed all the new approaches as beliefs and therapies came and went: *It's a problem with the bones... no, the discs... the muscles are at fault... no, the nerves are irritated... it's the patient's brain... their mindset is wrong...* and on and on.

Attending many courses—not wishing to fail or miss out on anything—I was happy to have these skills to diagnose a variety of problems but *fixing* them was another matter. The more I learned, the more frustrated I became, and ended up feeling I knew less than when I'd begun. For 15 years, I had been teaching postgraduates traditional ways of treating patients. I needed to pause and recalibrate, but money and family responsibilities kept me on the same track.

"Who has not sat before his own heart's curtain?
It lifts: and the scenery is falling apart."

– Rainer Maria Rilke

Physiotherapy

Physiotherapy is a science-based profession that helps people who are affected by injury, illness, and disability. Neuromuscular physiotherapy uses manual therapy—touching the body—to facilitate change by bringing awareness through the senses. We give specific movement and exercises to empower clients to trust and feel safe in their bodies and to use them as efficiently as possible. Listening deeply and offering advice is an integral part in the process of healing.

One physiotherapy teacher who I found particularly inspiring was Bob Elvey, a wonderful clinician from Australia. I had the privilege of studying with him in Perth for a year in 1991, when he showed me his way of dialoguing with the body. Bob was a man of few words, but it was more what he didn't say that intrigued me. His focus on *listening, feeling, and being* with the body—giving space for the body to bring forth its own answers—was unsurpassed and showed me that by doing less, clients often benefitted more. I brought home all I had learned and practiced, adding to the silent and invisible communications between myself and my patients. I experienced a deep satisfaction every time I was able to help a patient in his or her process of relieving the pain.

Successes notwithstanding, I came to a point when I still doubted the effectiveness of what I was doing. What was pain really about? I knew traditional medical science was limiting and didn't hold all the answers, so I decided to stop teaching and focus instead on *investigating*. I had no idea where it would lead me; I just knew I needed a degree of certainty in my practice and confidence in all areas of my life. I wanted answers.

The Healing Puzzle

"Where did the notion come from that we have to go to a doctor when we are sick anyway?"

– Bruce Lipton

Why do patients' digestive problems improve when I fix their painful backs? Why do skin issues appear and disappear for no apparent reason? I began to notice that when people's pain disappears, they are able to find new jobs and experience better relationships with their families and partners. They no longer need to be encouraged to lose weight or begin exercising, as they're naturally motivated to do it for themselves. It's as though nature or some newly released innate force is guiding them.

I greatly admire the work of David Butler, a physiotherapist in Adelaide, Australia, who is the founder of the Neuro Orthopaedic Institute. David wrote, "What bugs me is that it took so long to realise that it was I myself who was probably the main variable in outcomes—not the techniques."[3] Perhaps health professionals are, first and foremost, *catalysts* for change, a little like sprinkling stardust. Perhaps it's less what we do and more what we inspire and encourage. I was beginning to find more pieces to the healing puzzle.

Taking detailed histories from patients can be revealing and informative, but the information I receive is rarely what I would have imagined. Some people with a long list of conditions say that they're in good health, while others with a couple of minor ailments tell me they're quite ill. Why does one person feel a need to describe every element of their medical history, repeating it several times to be sure I've heard it all, while others just want solutions, keeping their descriptions short and to the point? Listening to what patients don't say, the spaces between their words, can be as insightful as what they tell me.

As I continued with my reading, coursework, and research, ideas began to take form. When we create a shift in the way we look at situations, we bring new possibilities into view. The patient along with the health professional together can determine healing recipes that have a greater likelihood of sustaining health and vitality.

Since childhood, I've been interested in the cultures and beliefs of people around the world, including indigenous healers—shamans, kāhuna, witch doctors, and curanderos—who help others to heal by expanding their own and their 'patients' awareness. Through ceremonial practices, they help engender a healing energy shift in the physical body. I realized this was an element of what I was looking for. Working in a circle with others facilitates the energy change. I first experienced this feeling of lightness, peace, and happiness of being while sitting around fires singing songs on a Christian holiday. This awareness of both togetherness and singularity stayed with me for a long while after each gathering.

---

[3] David Butler, "The Rollercoaster of Professional Life – still evolving," Neuro Orthopaedic Institute, accessed August 28, 2021, https://www.noigroup.com/noijam/the-rollercoaster-of-professional-life-still-evolving/.

I began to see that it is, in part, the healer's *presence* that determines the potential for *success*, and I began to see that having an agenda or a particular outcome in mind could limit results. Could I develop a better communication system *within myself* that would benefit the patient, an inner *conversation* that is more open and attuned to the healing rhythms presented? When I asked myself this, I *literally* heard the resounding sound of a bell from within and an encouraging "Yes, yes!" which I took as a call to listen to my own heart and innate wisdom.

With this new understanding and expanding awareness, I was able to engage fully with my heart and attune to the deeper experience of pain and emotional struggles within myself and my patients. This was a fundamental shift in how I now approach my work.

"We don't see things as they are.
We see them as we are."

– Anaïs Nin

Though I ran a private practice at that time, I was also commissioned by the UK National Health Service (NHS) to provide public services to local patients. Over the years, I'd been sending emails, leaflets, and other communications to healthcare providers, hoping to raise awareness of alternative techniques, telling them the anecdotal successes I had achieved using these therapies. I wanted the NHS to acknowledge the regenerative capabilities of the body.

Around eight years after my first Eureka moments, I was invited to attend a multidisciplinary conference on improving the musculoskeletal services in the region. It seemed a perfect opportunity to share with the NHS community, particularly the chronic pain teams, what I'd learned through my experiences with patients. Many orthopedic consultants and doctors from local hospitals attended the conference, along with other health professionals, including my colleagues in physiotherapy.

During the morning session, we identified areas for more in-depth discussion, areas needing improvement, and areas where too much money was being spent. The efficacy of the treatments was never talked about. We each chose a discussion group where we felt our own experience and knowledge could help improve the service. I wanted to join the participants of the section on chronic pain.

Even before we divided into groups, one of the service providers from the chronic pain team stood and gave a monologue on the merits of the service, stating that it did not need any improvements. I could barely believe my ears. My work schedule was filled with patients desperate to live pain-free. Many had been to "pain clinics" without relief and were told to manage and adjust their lives accordingly. Even the convener of the conference had spoken eloquently on the benefit of further input, but to no avail: The chronic pain discussion group never took place. This kind of defensive behavior is all too common in the healthcare community and fails to consider the needs of patients suffering from continuing pain who might benefit from new practices and therapies.

I wanted greater freedom in the choice of services I could offer my patients, so early in 2015 I contacted the NHS commissioner who monitored my contract to see if he would be open to suggestions about new ways to reach those who had not been helped by existing therapies. I offered anecdotal evidence that the inclusion of alternative modalities such as meditation and reflection had been beneficial for chronic pain patients. A lengthy email correspondence ensued, followed by a request that I research evidence from reviews deemed trustworthy by the NHS and to send them to him. I did just that and pointed out that the employees of Public Health England had access to a free mindfulness app. Sadly, it all fell on deaf ears. I received an email telling me that I was wasting his time and should not continue in that vein. So, reluctantly, I left the NHS, handing over the clinic I had built up over twenty-five years to begin working with clients in ways that incorporated my new understanding, and to pursue my research. I wanted to be part of a paradigm shift in how we view the process of healing.

One of the saddest elements was leaving my loyal colleagues in the clinic. Together we had formed a harmonious, supportive team, a community helping people change their lives. The clinic was on the edge of the English Channel, a changing seascape with France often visible just 21 miles across the water. In the warmer months we took ocean dips at lunchtime to refresh ourselves before our afternoon work. In the winter we let the strong southwesterly winds blow through us clearing any tensions we held. I'll never forget the many happy years working with the sound of the ocean nearby and the taste and smell of fresh, salty air.

Changing Scenes/Regeneration

"Life is a process of becoming, a combination of states we have to go through. Where people fail is that they wish to elect a state and remain in it. This is a kind of death."

– Anaïs Nin

I set out to discover a simple process that could empower others to know themselves and feel alive, a process that could help people remember their own source of power to facilitate changes in their bodies and their lives. I knew that science and our innate healing power could work hand in hand. We evolve and regenerate through listening to ourselves and to creation's higher wisdom.

I moved from a mechanical, medicine-based treatment approach to one that involves playful inventing, transforming energy, and working with ancient spiritual wisdom and love. As my perspectives shifted, I began to meet many wonderful teachers, and these women and men continue to show me the art of communicating within one's own body, mind, and spirit.

The concept of co-creative wisdom evolved from opening a welcoming space to dialogue with the physical energy exchange of the body and developing the skill of inner listening. I discovered that, without any thought or logical thinking, pain can be transformed in these exchanges. All the answers we need are within, and as we become aware of the questions to ask, the answers will reveal themselves.

As this process, which I've come to name Concentra, has unfolded, I've experienced the language of nature, changed my diet, left my marriage, changed my career, sold my business, experienced wisdom from the spirit world, and travelled. As a consequence, I have created greater space both within myself and outside.

Did I plan for any of this? Not exactly. But I dared to look outside the reality I was holding. I listened to the silence, came to enjoy the stillness, and became conscious of how awareness changes. Within this creative process of becoming, lost in the mystery of transformation, I found myself anew—again and again. I discovered that medicine and spirituality walk hand in hand, and in the process, I became both participant and observer of death and creation unfolding.[4]

[4] My definition of spirituality is an awareness that encourages the spirit of humanness, that the breath we all share is an equal integral part of existence just as much as the visible material world that we live in. The unseen transformative forces are as real as the visible ones.

Part 2

Pain and the Human Body

Chapter 2

Pain Unmasked

"We are shaped and fashioned by what we love."

– Johann Wolfgang von Goethe

What Is Pain?

Pain is an elusive sensation that no one has been able to see, measure, or capture on camera or with any instrument, despite decades of research. It comes in many forms and is sometimes difficult even to identify. It's not composed of solid matter—no atoms or electrons—or anything that can be quantified scientifically. We can measure the *effects* of pain by how it impinges upon our ability to live our lives and carry out physical activities, but as yet we are no closer to finding the *essence of pain*. It changes form, quantity, and quality. It comes and goes as if by magic: a trickster, or master magician.

Is pain a *concept*, an experience created for us to engage, learn from, and play with? Is pain an invitation to explore our wondrous inner being, a pointer for us to know ourselves better? I believe that it is. Let us open this conversation.

Pain is a doorway into ourselves, a place for us to know ourselves better.

Acute pain is an essential experience alerting us to potential damage to our physical body. Pain may tell us to seek urgent medical attention. In the case of a broken bone or a sprained ligament, it's a wonderful protective mechanism that forces us to stop using the places and parts that hurt, and to rest. But what if the pain lingers and does not go away as expected? What is chronic or persistent pain trying to tell us after the damaged tissues have healed? Perhaps it's an unconscious choice we make to halt our return to wellness, our preference to stay with the familiar, even if uncomfortable, rather than address the deeper healing that is being called for.

How many of us have had symptoms, followed by blood tests and x-rays, and the results come back as normal? The pain or disease can't be explained through microscopic analysis or abnormal anatomy. Diagnoses like functional neurosis, syndromes, or atypical seronegative rheumatoid arthritis may be given. Some doctors seem to diagnose unexplained symptoms as unknown or unknowable, or "You're fine." Other specialists hedge their bets, placing larger wagers on some ideas over others. Some request additional and ongoing tests. Sometimes there's just no box that fits you or your symptoms.

Many of my patients with discomfort and even agony are unaware of the cause of their pain. If all problems originated solely from the physical body, all pain could be addressed mechanically. We would see for example, pain worsen when performing a specific movement, or subside when lying in a certain position. But often there is no clear cause. A patient might report experiencing pain at night when the body is resting or when she is enjoying a few quiet moments to herself. Why does something hurt one minute and then is fine the next? Sometimes the body produces a pain that seems random or spontaneous. But what if it's not random? What if we simply aren't conscious of the triggers?

I suggest that we experience pain when the awareness of our physical body becomes disorganized. It also presents an opportunity to recalibrate again. The intangible nature of the pain creates a space for us to explore and discover something that is hidden. It's asking to communicate with us. When we observe the pain with our wisdom, pay attention to the images that come up and the sensations we feel, new threads may be revealed. Pain becomes a signal to listen and unravel. When seen and felt with fresh perception, pain may reorganize in its own way.

Pain is, in my experience, a sign for us to listen, release its binds, and allow the space for a new connection. When we release our focus from the *disharmony* within, we may again feel the comfort and pleasure of inhabiting our bodies.

> *Pain is an awareness of something that is not in harmony with the oneness of self, nature, and the Divine.*

A young, female patient's symptoms gave me insight into the idea that there was more to pain than purely tissue damage. She presented with an 18 month history of disabling wrist and hand pain, unable to work or perform any household task for more than 15 minutes. She'd been diagnosed with repetitive strain injury (RSI). During our initial consultation, she became irate—swearing, shaking her painful hands and arms, and blaming doctors and others. I couldn't get a word in, so I let her rant, telling me all the problems she'd been experiencing. It was clear she needed to vent. When she eventually paused, I commented that she seemed frustrated and angry, cornered, and trapped by her situation. She felt heard, that I understood how she was feeling, and she allowed herself to release more of her pent-up anger. Additional complaining ensued, and when she arrived for her next session two weeks later, she told me she felt much better in herself, and she could hold objects and was able to do more tasks around the home.

This was an 'Ah-ha' moment for me. I realized that it's not solely physical, biological, chemical, or neurological systems that are responsible for manifestations of pain in the body. If expressing your feelings changes sensations and the level of pain, it means these sensations are there for a reason. So I began to look for solutions in how the pain was being expressed through the patient rather than attempting to define or even fix the pain. By shifting our perspective on the perceived problem and listening to our bodies (and by the therapist listening to what the patient is saying), we can receive insights and recognize connections. And sometimes then the pain patterns simply release.

Why Does Pain Linger?

If you're in a car crash, or receive unexpected news that someone has died, or experience any other physical, emotional, or mental trauma, the memory imprint will likely become stuck in the body. The pain momentarily disrupts the flow of life's continuum by overwhelming us. We may even exit from our bodies. Traumatic shock can express in muscle tension or resistance, chronic pain, compromised immunity, or a host of other symptoms. We might hold our breath from fear or experience a most uncomfortable physical sensation. Everyone experiences pain differently.

And please note that it's common to experience *more* pain days or even weeks after an event, rather than right after it. If any part of the energy body remains disorganized, we're likely to continue experiencing problems until the trauma has been felt and integrated. The body heals specific areas in a systematic sequencing during our return to wholeness.

We are only conscious of something that has not been integrated into awareness.

When significant emotional events take hold, many factors coalesce and challenge the conscious mind to create stories about what happened. Or sometimes, we simply blank it out. Our minds and bodies carry the imprints of our unique survival circuitry and if we don't know or notice it, we're likely to continue our daily lives with the discordant energy stored within.

What happens if, while we're in pain, other events delay our ability to release the trapped energy and the tissues stop healing part way through the repair process? If we ignore the communication of pain that our body gives us inviting us to reconnect to healing, the trauma may become even more deeply embedded. The natural healing process of the body becomes hijacked by feelings of stress and overwhelm. We begin to tune ourselves to a different rhythm, unable to find the reset button. Unless we intentionally look within and align ourselves with the natural patterns of healing—finding coherence and balance with our feedback systems—we will not experience sustained relief from the symptoms.

The Experience of Pain

The individual manifestation of pain is a unique pattern involving memory and may include a sensation, feeling, emotion, or thought which can be sensed through the visual, auditory, olfactory, taste, pressure, or touch dimensions. All memories are time-dependent and with experience, we can become aware of the presence of the gravitational and directional forces sustaining a memory's existence. For example, a person may have tinnitus when she looks to the left, but not when she looks to the right. Or a person may feel certain emotions like sadness when he looks down, but not when he looks up.

CASE STUDY
Gwen has a conversation with her ankle

An elderly patient, Gwen, came to me complaining of persistent ankle pain. While I was examining the area, she became agitated and sat up quickly as if ready for a fight. I realized this was no ordinary sprained ankle, so I decided to take another approach.

"Share with me some more details," I requested. She explained that approximately four months earlier she'd been walking along the canal path chatting to her friend when without warning, she stumbled in a hole. It was a shock and she hadn't been able to walk since, except with a walking stick.

> *"When did you last have a shock like that, out of the blue?" I queried.*
>
> *Without a moment's hesitation, her eyes fixed on mine and she said, "When the consultant told my husband his cancer had come back. We'd been expecting good news."*
>
> *Immediately after she spoke those words, her ankle began to move. I continued to examine it, this time with no painful response from Gwen. The healing energy was free to move again, the body was starting to reorganize. The ankle injury had been connected in Gwen's memory with the shock of the consultant's unexpected words about the reoccurrence of her husband's cancer. The intensity of this past memory had contributed significantly to her ongoing pain. After actively remembering this emotional event while I was helping to release her ankle, Gwen was able to dissociate the pain of these two events. She walked out of the treatment room visualizing the future with a spring in her step, the stick no longer needed.*

Energetic discord can become stuck in any part of the body, for example in our immune, cardiovascular, musculoskeletal, lymphatic, or hormonal systems. We experience pain whenever the misaligned part of the energy is triggered by a movement, a thought, a belief, or even an environmental trigger such as a person, place, or smell. New pains can merge with other systems already operating and, before you know it, all the symptoms become part of the same program and body map of experience and expression.

Over time, it's possible to experience almost anything: whole body pain such as fibromyalgia, pain and swelling with tiredness such as chronic fatigue and chronic regional pain syndrome, symptoms after eating a healthy meal like irritable bowel syndrome, and even anxiety when everything is going well. Any configuration is possible.

This body of symptoms—syndromes as they're often called—don't fit well with a medical model that divides the body into parts and hands out diagnostic labels. It is far more fruitful to see our bodies as dynamic, interconnected systems that are continually responding to environmental changes inside and outside the body through the languages of energy and information. Our body is our personal barometer.

The Danger of Diagnoses

If pain becomes a thing, an object with a label like a diagnosis, it appears more concrete, a material structure with fixed boundaries, and this can engender a continuous pain experience.[5] We experience sensory changes, such as numbness, and shut ourselves off from the experience. We develop heightened sensitivity in the area of pain and other areas of our body to protect ourselves. These sensations are given medical names like allodynia, hypersensitivity, and dysesthesia, which reinforces the idea that it is something and beyond our control.

Emotions can swing uncontrollably, and a feeling of overwhelm may fill our heads with unhelpful thoughts and scenarios. We may determine that moving the part of our body with the pain is dangerous and guard movement with our muscles. Any and all combinations of thoughts, beliefs, and sensations are possible in this experience of pain. We may unconsciously choose not to engage fully with it, which results in a static or stuck situation.

---

[5] Daniel Jonah Friedman, Louise Tulloh, Karim M Khan, "Peeling off musculoskeletal labels: sticks and stones may break my bones, but diagnostic labels can hamstring me forever," *British Journal of Sports Medicine* Epub ahead of print: (06 May 2021), doi: 10.1136/bjsports-2021-103998.

Anxiety and anticipation are echoes of what we believe may happen.

If we listen to professional advice or the counsel of friends and family, we may feel the need for protection. We look up our pains on the internet only to discover that we're suffering from even more than we'd thought. Media outlets love scare stories, and we're told endlessly how to live and what's best for our health. We allow ourselves to feel disempowered, that we're getting older, or incapacitated, and we fall into resignation, forgetting the amazing design and healing capacity of the human body.

Diagnostic imaging such as magnetic resonance imaging (MRI) scans and x-rays are used to match symptoms with findings. Even though much evidence suggests that these correlations are inaccurate, it explains the problem and we think we're stuck with the pain. The scan proved it—we saw it. I have supported hundreds of patients to accept a different reality about their crumbling backs, bulging discs, and degenerating bodies, which helped to shift the *forever pain* experience into *never again*. If we believe there is nothing to protect, it is easier to listen to and trust your body's capacity to heal. Pain is not fixed or terminal. It changes with loving and wise attention.

When we release rigid ideas about pain and health prognoses, loosen our frames of reference and focus simply on an intent and desire to get better, resources spontaneously appear. A diagnosis can provide a handle to grip onto and provide stability as we create a personal plan of recovery. Be careful though that the label doesn't separate the body from its inherent desire of returning to wholeness. Instead, use pain as an opening to new experiences lifting you to new heights of awareness.

"When you change the way you look at things,
the things you look at change."

– Max Planck

Our Unconscious Pain Narrative

We build walls around us by the stories we tell ourselves, our beliefs and internal chatter. We anticipate pain, and these expectations affect our behavior. We brace ourselves before feeling anything as if we're already in pain. Perhaps we experienced back pain when unloading the washing machine or picking up a suitcase, and now all forward movements feel like they're a threat. Some patients experience pain on the same date each year, perhaps on an anniversary for something. I've found that patients' pain sometimes disappears once they've booked an appointment; just anticipating the relief, their bodies begin to heal.

We may unconsciously choose to suffer rather than to *accept* the pain and *watch* it change. The pain may represent a justification for being angry with our boss or blaming the person who hit our car. I've seen people angry with their bodies for letting them down, for not giving them a second chance. Who then benefits? Who continues to experience loss and abandonment? Pain disappears when we can accept, forgive, and love our bodies again.

Pain challenges us to feel the very things we fear that, at the same time, will help us the most.

CASE STUDY
What Sarah's knee wanted to tell her

Sarah was a 51-year-old hospital employee. She had suffered a severe injury to her left knee three years earlier and since then had been suffering from pain, swelling, and heat in her joint. She fell on it once again and had three operations and then a knee replacement.

She continued to experience pain, with visible inflammatory changes that led to yet another operation to remove the synovium (the membrane of her knee), and there was still no change in her pain experience. She was off work, walked with a limp, was in constant pain with muscle weakness and restricted movement.

I noticed that Sarah was not 'connecting' with her leg and asked if she'd had a problem with her left pelvic area. "I had an operation that went badly, and now my groin is numb."

I suggested she try to feel this area, and she said she'd chosen to blank out the problem in her pelvis and would prefer not to feel it. We discussed the benefits at length, and I encouraged her to try to reconnect with that part of her body.

She was not keen to follow my advice and told me so. However, on retesting the hypersensitivity in her knee, the pain and swelling had already started to reduce. I gave her some exercises and suggested she consider ways she might pay more attention to her leg again and become friends with it. As she was leaving, she said she wanted to feel feminine and wear high heels again.

At her second appointment two weeks later, Sarah said the exercises hadn't worked. I asked how her knee was, and she responded, "I'm doing water aerobics three times a week, exercises from another physiotherapist, and will have a session of lymph drainage. I decided not to be a victim, and my knee is starting to feel better."

At the end of our session. Sarah told me she'd gone out the previous evening and worn her wedge shoes. I hid my smile at this change of events and the positive move toward her desire to be more 'feminine.' Despite her belief that the exercises I'd suggested had not helped, I witnessed the change. She did not return to me for treatment again.

Once we open to the possibility of healing and move across the threshold, resources and ideas arise to help us. By feeling, observing, and dialoguing with the pain and the lost connection it represents, we become free to live, think, and breathe anew. Most important is to be open, flexible, and creative in our desire to heal.

Changing Our Relationship with Pain

How can we access unhelpful pain patterns and then rewire them? The pain memories are stored in our unconscious, a unique time capsule, and talking about them may not be enough to realize the remedy. We don't need endless stories from the past or analytical interpretation—that may only satisfy our egos. In fact, some talking therapies embroider the same wiring, as the pattern is relived and replayed again and again. Thought loops and pain itself can become addictions. Wise therapists shine the light of awareness on the healing connections so that the discordant emotional and mental patterns are revealed. Open and willing hearts bring that into focus and support the desire for a more intimate relationship with all parts of the self.

Some people use pain as a measure of how successful they've been, how tough, how much they can endure suffering. It becomes addictive. Pain becomes a kind of pleasure, the scales out of balance. Unwittingly, we choose to suffer. It's familiar, known. The art is to become aware of that moment that both binds us to and frees us from the pain, and then ride that wave to equilibrium and stand firmly on our own two feet again.

CASE STUDY
Mark talks to his whole body

Mark was a retired soldier. At the beginning of our session, he spoke for 20 minutes about his diagnoses and the many areas of pain in his body. As he paused to see my response, I reflected and asked, "Which of your ailments troubles you the most?"

He identified his hot, swollen, and painful ankle. I asked him to feel the ankle and describe his relationship with it. He voiced his beliefs around why the pain was there, what it prevented him from doing, his discharge from the army, and his inability to run. He didn't know what he would do after being in the military his whole adult life. All the while, I was gently massaging and moving the foot so he could experience new sensations and witness the foot move differently.

After ten or so minutes, he entered into a more comfortable relationship with that part of his body. The ankle began to normalize, changing color and temperature. He was in awe of the seemingly miraculous change that had taken place after having the pain for such a long time. He put his foot on the ground tentatively and felt a new experience which he liked.

By the end of the treatment session, Mark had begun to realize that his relationship with this pain was not supporting his wish to move on with his life. He told me of his future plans and I sensed his desire and excitement about reaching his goals. I urged him to work with his symptoms to manifest his dreams.

To remember what is most important, most sacred to us, we need to be present with ourselves and release the resistance to the pain. It can help to revisit that formless, timeless place where we feel lost and vulnerable, for it will reveal all of its magic, healing, and wisdom. Becoming aware of the gap between our thoughts can be the catalyst to opening into a new experience, free from pain.

"The best and most beautiful things in the world
cannot be seen or even touched.
They must be felt by the heart."

– Helen Keller

When a new dawn of awareness arises, you decide whether it is true for you, seeing an action you can take in that moment, knowing you are free to change your mind again and again. You are the one who knows what you are looking for.

CASE STUDY
A conversation with Michael

Michael came to me complaining of headaches and neck pain following a whiplash injury three years earlier.

"I don't understand," he said. "It was only a minor jolt at the time; I've had worse injuries that didn't persist this long."

He had tried physiotherapy before and had taken painkilling medications but was still in pain.

I placed my hands on his head and neck, and Michael started to feel the tightness there and throughout his body. Within five minutes, he felt safe enough to release the rigidity in his arms. He had an instantaneous memory of holding the steering wheel and gear stick during the accident and of the fear he felt of never being able to move again. In my office that day, his desire to let go released the disharmonious neural patterns and he stretched his body out in the opposite direction from the injury. We continued deeper into the release work, working on other areas of his body.

Ten days later Michael returned, smiling: "My neck pain is gone and the headaches too. I've been taking painkillers for back pain for 20 years and I don't need them now. I feel like a different person. I've even begun making plans to rejoin the judo club."

Michael's seemingly unrelated back pain from so many years earlier was connected to the more recent whiplash problems. When we dialogue with the symptoms, in this case the 'locked-up pain' and give them a voice, they often just fade away.
I've witnessed many similar healings. As we become more mindful, we can see how certain situations appear repeatedly for our benefit and regeneration. Neither Michael nor I knew that this whiplash 'doorway' would also bring about healing for his lower spine and his overall sense of well-being. In his own words, he was now able to 'move again.' I did not enquire to the relevance of this statement, but it was a key that led to his healing.

Faith in Our Capacity to Heal

The power of the so-called placebo effect has measurable and potent health responses. The medical definition for the term placebo is anything that seems to be a real medical treatment but isn't deemed to be. For example, giving an injection of salt water instead of a painkiller, cutting open a knee joint and closing it again without performing any procedure, or giving a sugar pill instead of an antidepressant. Research trials have shown the substantial benefits that occur with a "fake" therapeutic intervention. Even the color of the placebo tablet has a unique measurable effect on the response of the person. What is the science behind this?

We can all invest in the innate wisdom of our bodies. This trust can be harnessed by our own belief and knowing that something will help us, even when there's a mystery about how. We can give ourselves the green light to tap into the healing system. We are the ones who put limits on the capacity of our bodies to heal at a given moment. We can call an unexplained positive response a placebo or a miracle.

In most research papers, the placebo effect is not given the credence it warrants, and it's often hidden or included in the effectiveness of a drug. The constant in all clinical trials, though, is that the placebo effect carries great value. It's not an error. As much as 50 percent of the improvement with any medical intervention can be attributed to a placebo response, a miracle, or an individual's innate ability to tap into the healing energy. The question then is if it is so powerful, how can this effect be harnessed with or without the use of the medicines or other traditional medical treatments?

The Brain, Pain, and Consciousness

We use brain imaging techniques, such as electroencephalography (EEG) and magnetic resonance imaging (MRI) scans, to look at potential health issues. The output—the picture and recording—is compared with what is agreed upon as normal, and areas that don't fit with that are highlighted and given great weight, sometimes more than may be warranted.

Our bodies, including our brains, are always in a relationship with the cosmic sea of consciousness, the non-local universal field of quantum information and infinite potentialities. MRI scans of the brains of monks who excel in meditation show more extensive interconnectedness and neural coordination of the whole brain, with the 'happier' areas showing more active.[6] Is it that the monks are reflecting a greater relationship with the spaciousness and potentialities of the universe and this is registered in the MRI we see? Their scans display more freedom of communication within the brain structure. In patients where a structural anomaly is discovered such as a tumor, this unusual area of electromagnetic activity is a reflection of a different type of relationship.

When we intentionally look to make new connections, we experience structural changes, and new realities are observable in our bodies. Sometimes just a slight adjustment of our internal state will bring ourselves into alignment with different external forces of energy. These perfectly matching potentials can spark the energy of miracles.

The conscious mind on its own does not have a great capacity for change. Positive thinking and willpower certainly help, but the innate, pure order of Divine creation in you flows fully by letting go of the tight reins that guide the mind around and around in the same-sized circles. It is only then that you truly experience healing. When you take a moment to look and rest inside your

---

[6] Fadel Zeidan, Katherine T. Martucci, Robert A. Kraft et al, "Brain Mechanisms Supporting the Modulation of Pain by Mindfulness Meditation," *Journal of Neuroscience* 31, no. 14, (April 2011): 5540–5548.

body, you will find there is nothing to mend, fix, or change. As we accept and 'live' the inside as the outside, attuning to the impermanent and creative flow of life, our health benefits. When we can release any resistance to this flow, this ever-changing rhythm, we can then start to live in the state of expanded potential, perhaps similar to what the monks experience in their practices.

The Body as the Link to Consciousness

As individuals with consciousness, we have the ability to take in information from the world around us and embody it in our physical being. How we assimilate information about our environment can transform our physical bodies. 'Ah-ha' moments arise as new levels of awareness facilitate a restructuring of energy within our bodies and our consciousness. Our eyes, ears, nose, tongue, and whole body take in sensations of the world in all its dimensions. As they enter our body and mind, we give meaning to our world in the experiences of beauty and connection, or ugliness and separation. We flow with life as we observe, touch, listen to, taste, and smell all that life has to offer. We can choose to see it all though rose-tinted glasses or observe the rawness of what we encounter, without distortion.

We awaken to life by experiencing all we encounter, including both pleasure and pain. Some people experience the world mostly through sight, others sound, taste, smell, language, or touch. We are each a unique mix of the senses and experience our holographic world through these blending patterns, our infinite 'recipe of sensory experience.' With pain that is associated with a traumatic event, the more the individual can connect to the memory of that event through all the five senses, the more complete the healing. As we deepen and open our connection to the universe, we discover previously hidden communication systems that heighten our appreciation of life.

Some individuals are born with synesthesia which is a blending of the senses. For example, they might smell something that you and I can only see. I had a client who was able to smell the plant when I was showing her pictures of only the flowers. Tasting words and hearing music with numbers is also possible.

Sensations of our environment do not happen in isolation, and yet, if we experienced everything through each of our senses all together, it might be too much for our system to process. These kinds of experiences can happen in those who have taken plant medicine or other hallucinogenic substances without the correct preparation. I remember picking oranges from my uncle's tree in Spain when I was young. I loved the scent they gave and to this day when I peel an orange or grate its zest, I recall the pleasure I took from the smell of that newly harvested orange and the vision of seeing it on the tree under the warmth and light of the sun. I had a similar experience when holidaying in Sri Lanka. I smelled and tasted fresh cinnamon bark we had cut from the tree. It was exquisitely sweet and juicy in my mouth, and I felt the delight all over my body. Taste too can be a multisensory experience.

Next time you hear the wind smell it, taste it, see it, and feel it.

When we pay attention to our limbs, we notice how the joint angles change actioned by the muscles. Receptors in the muscles and joints feed into our nervous system, giving us internal feedback on what is happening in the whole of the muscular system. This receptor activity gives constant feedback about the outside environment. The balance or imbalance between relaxation and contraction, tension and release of the muscles is registered. Information from the receptors helps to determine the optimal force and specific movement for that particular activity.

This ability to feel where our body is and how it is moving is called *proprioception*. We combine these internal sensations with sensations of our external environment to align our bodies with the outside world. Are we standing straight and equally on both legs? Are we leaning backwards or forwards? We know this by comparing information from the outside with these sensations from the inside. When our bodies perceive these two as incongruent, or out of phase, it is reflected in our outward appearance. We feel unstable, lean forward, or hang on tightly to stay on our feet. If we observe ourselves from all directions, the mismatch shifts and we re-center ourselves on the path.

Losing your balance after suddenly hearing something unexpected is an example of reduced sensory integration. Perhaps hearing a noise makes you feel sick. I was helping a patient with a digestive problem and as I moved her neck she began to feel nauseous. This continued until she consciously let go of the tension around her jaw. She had suddenly remembered her father saying to her, "You were born dizzy."

To reboot the way we orient to the world, we need first to accept the possibility of change. From there, we can choose to change the way we experience things. Our mind and body need to talk to and experience each other.

The Place of Pain without Medication

We've learned to turn away from our bodies through medication. When we try to 'fix a problem' solely with pills, we prevent ourselves from journeying to the other side of the 'hiccup' to a new experience of mind and body. Prolonged use of antidepressants, opiates, or anti-inflammatories prevents full engagement with ourselves and affects those around us. We lock ourselves in a cage, losing the key and endlessly spinning like a hamster on its wheel. By avoiding or ignoring our symptoms, we prevent solutions from arising. Alternatively, we can choose to 'live with it' for a while, with or without medication, and this is sometimes helpful. At some point, if we can then learn to embrace our inner resources and dialogue with the body, we may learn something from our situation. Sometimes this requires patience and persistence; sometimes the results are immediate. Once we experience the shift, we know it's repeatable. But it's not guaranteed that we will choose differently, even after knowing there are alternatives. The patterns of our defense circuitry can be strong, and we may continue to keep something at arm's length, believing it might be too painful to let in.

Using the vast seas of informational energy, self-compassion, and love all around us we can integrate all the separate parts that make up the symptoms of our pain. Reconnection happens in a place of 'non-doing,' when we listen to the body's intelligent communication systems as they receive and translate the consciousness of the universe.

CASE STUDY
Healing the "separate islands"

Joyce, aged 70, came to see me with headaches and severe back pain. She also suffered from psoriasis on her scalp, a condition that produces red bumpy patches that are covered with white scale. She'd had this problem since her son suddenly died a year earlier. He had died in Australia, and she had not been able to see him before his passing.

Using touch techniques to move the energy and release tight fascia, muscles, and joints, and dialoguing with her about her awareness of the pain, she alleviated the headaches and the scalp itching. Over a few sessions, Joyce moved through her fear, loss, and grief by engaging with the parts of her body that had symptoms and had asked to be seen. She was able to let go of the shock around her son's death, the unpleasant vision she had of him under the ground, and some of the loss she felt. By breathing into the areas of her body with the symptoms and observing her body's sensations, she harnessed the body's inner strength and healing wisdom, and she began to flow again with the energy of the universe.

After several sessions, Joyce finally felt confident that she could schedule urgently needed eye surgery without worrying that the head itching would cause her to move her head. Perhaps the problem with the eyes was also a reflection of the trauma she had experienced?

Being Playful with Pain

Pain can reduce temporarily, or at least move out of our conscious awareness, when our minds engage in other things. When this happens, we feel so much better, as our bodies run on different neural patterns. This experience is beneficial for us for it reminds us that our pain is not permanent, however neither is it the whole solution.

I heard about a man who was bilingual, and when he spoke in one language he experienced continual pain, and when he spoke in the other, he felt no pain at all. When we have one hat on, our blood sugar may run high, and yet another, it normalizes. Compare your personality at home with who you are at work or driving your kids to school. What does this tell us? We have the ability to run multiple programs.

We can also use our imagination to connect with and align with our pain and feel its release. A play therapist told me about a little boy who was unhappy at home, and angry and disruptive at school. He was able to work through his anger by playing with cars on a toy racing track. At first the cars crashed and never completed a circuit. Fallen trees, boulders, and other cars blocked the way. Eventually he found the space within himself to let all the cars finish the race. With every completed lap, the victory flag waved. His behavior improved in school, and he became more involved with his classes and his classmates.

When we use play to engage with a situation, it can bring lightness, focus, and expansion at the same time. Combining these dynamic principles can dissolve tension, bringing harmony and resolution to many kinds of situations.

Self-Compassion: Choosing a Fresh Path

One way to remove the pain forever is to find a new truth: Change the reality of the perceived problem. Open to another direction or possibility from a place of self-compassion, gratitude, and love. Focus on your intent to bring flow into your life again. Ignoring your pain, diverting the mind, being constantly angry, going to sleep, giving it over to another to fix, or running away from it provides no permanent solution. Accept and thank your body for the experience of pain as a way of helping you to become aligned and free again.

Begin by looking for clues in the ways you express yourself. Are your words kind? Does the kindness extend to yourself and to others?

How often have you had one or more of these thoughts?

- "I feel like I've been stabbed in the back."
- "I can't take a full breath in. It feels as though someone is sitting on my chest."
- "I have a huge irritation under my skin."
- "I hate myself."
- "I have no support around me."
- "I don't feel like I can move forward."
- "There is a missed communication."
- "My brain feels like mush."
- "I must be wrong."
- "My body is always failing me."
- "I feel like I'm wired up all wrong."
- "Why does nothing go right?"

CASE STUDY
What were Joan's headaches a re-membering of?

Joan walked into the treatment room using a cane and holding onto her husband's arm. She was a talkative and fit 72 years old. "I can't stand these headaches anymore and neither can my husband. They stop us from enjoying so many things. I get annoyed because I feel unsteady and I have to hold his arm and it is getting worse."

Joan was obviously fed up with her headaches and decreasing lack of stability and mobility for they took away her ability to participate fully in life. After I had assessed her physical function, she lay down on the couch. As I was examining her neck and head she suddenly became frightened. "There's a steamroller coming toward me. It's going to squash me," she exclaimed, her voice quivering.

I helped her stay focused and calm by connecting to my breath, heart, and body. "How do you want to save yourself?" I asked.

"I'm making the driver put on the brake, and it's stopping," she replied.

She had found her own way out of her life-threatening situation. She was obviously ripe and ready to change.

The next time Joan came to see me, her headaches had stopped and she no longer needed a cane as her balance had improved so much. She walked briskly around the room, proud of the change she had made.

Joan had had epilepsy since she was four years old. With epilepsy, the brain misfires and intermittently gets stuck on a program that causes an imbalance in the brainwaves. It had been well-controlled with medication her whole life.

Joan told me that when she was four, she had been enjoying practising her new skill of bicycling. She had just recently been able to balance without stabilisers but had skidded on the grit left by a steamroller. The epilepsy had started shortly after this traumatic incident. Somewhere deep in her unconscious mind, the memory of the fear of her bicycle accident was still stored. When Joan had the vision of the steamroller during our session, I would have suggested she roll out of the way. But her remedy was different, and one's own vision or thought or solution is always the best one. Joan created her own healing story, reconnecting to the time, or times, she had become paralyzed with fear, and she herself released them.

This was an inspiring, spontaneous moment that taught me so much about the body's ability to heal no matter how long ago the energy of the problem had been embedded.

Open Your Treasure Chest

If we look at how our body works in a fresh way that is completely our own, tuning in to the messages from within, we can experience our body's treasures. Peek in, take a good look at the precious jewels inside, embrace all the glistening potentials. Breathe them into being, turning everything that you find beautiful to life, like the hero who slays the dragon and lives, eager for another day. With the help of those gems, author your own story, add more chapters, delete others, change the ending. It is you who puts a lid over the sparkles, and it's you that lifts the lid up to reveal your own precious rainbows.

"Where your treasure is, there will your heart be also."

– Matthew 6:21

Once you have experienced the magic, designed and played the part in your own show, you'll find that you can stage-manage anything, even when you're the only one left in the theater.

"Many of us spend our lives running from feeling with the
mistaken belief that you cannot bear the pain.
But you have already borne the pain.
What you have not done is feel all you are beyond the pain."

– Kahlil Gibran

Thoughts to Germinate

- Open to your persistent pain and health issue and curiously explore it.
- Pain does not always indicate that the physical body is damaged.
- Feel the interconnectedness of the body rather than viewing it as separate parts.
- Listen to your guiding inner voice and to the loving support that surrounds you.
- Believe you can heal and that the help you need is already present.
- Empower yourself to know the true healing wisdom of your body.
- Empowering yourself ignites the potential in others.
- It only takes an instant to start a chain reaction of connective healing. Be the first domino.

Chapter 3

The Subtle Energies That Shape Us

"We are perceivers. We are an awareness; we are not objects; we have no solidity. We are boundless."

– Don Juan, speaking to Carlos Castaneda

Is our body only matter, like a machine with one known set of instructions held by the medical establishment? From my years of experience, this linear, mechanical, and material model is incomplete. It's possible to change what happens inside the body and how we experience it if we're open to believing in other ways. If we do, we'll discover our unique, personal owner's manual.

How do yoga practitioners stay warm even when covered by a wet sheet and surrounded by snow? How are advanced Buddhist practitioners able to become the 'rainbow body' after death, their bodies not decaying but gradually shrinking and disappearing, leaving only hair and nails? I'm not suggesting you undertake these extreme practices, but use these to illustrate that our capabilities are far greater than we may have imagined.

A mystery only remains a mystery if we've forgotten what we already know.

Diseases are dynamic, ongoing processes, never static or stuck. With such fluid experiences we can participate in choosing the outcomes. The perspective we bring to all our encounters contributes to our experience of them, and this holds true for health and disease. Sometimes what we witness seems miraculous, which simply means we are not yet able to understand or measure with our instruments, or even our five senses, what has actually taken place.

Disease comes from our accumulated untruths about relationships.

I use the term cure to mean that a symptom is no longer present. When we heal, on the other hand, we reconnect our body to our sense of wholeness and innate wellness, empowering ourselves in this process, in essence a new relationship with the self. A 'cure' can thus be a hindrance to healing. If we cover over a symptom, we have no access to its message or to a correcting course, and we experience no meaningful, heartfelt awareness of the situation wanting our attention.

A woman with the diagnosis of Lou Gehrig's disease coined the term "Small Print Club" to describe her membership in the small percentage of people who are able to continue living healthily with this condition. She is an example of someone who defied the statistics and is maintaining healing connections, for after 14 years with the diagnosis she is still enjoying life to the fullest. I am sure we all know or have heard of cases like this. When we feel alive, we can appreciate what an incredible tuning fork our body has for life.

We will now look at how the cells, their membranes, and our DNA, contribute to our health and our relationship with our external environment.

Our Body's Unique Vision of the Rainbow

DNA – Deoxyribonucleic Acid and our Divine Natural Arrangement

The structure of DNA is a pair of twisting chains and this spiraling pattern is a form seen in many places in nature. The spiral of a shell and the seed head of a sunflower are also wonderful examples of the materialized energies of the universe. The unique DNA spiral communicates directly with vibrational information in our environment through resonance; it is in constant relationship with the infinite, dynamic and creative order of energy around us. Our unique sequences of DNA have the ability to respond to internal and external energy and stimuli, much like an antenna receives and transmits signals. Our unique strands may be continually shaped by cosmic information as they have been throughout evolution.[7] The body as a navigational tool is one of the most reliable and sensitive feedback systems we have. It is at our disposal every minute of the night and day.

Structurally, DNA is two parallel strands running in opposite directions which allows for the storage of three-dimensional data. In one cell of our bodies, the uncoiled DNA is six-and-a-half feet in length. If all the DNA in all our cells were attached end to end, they would circle the entire solar system twice. During an eight-year study, Dr. Peter Gariaev discovered that our DNA is a complex, biological, micro-computer chip that responds to the syntax of language, words, and prayers and is constantly moving under the influence of light photons.[8] Therefore, our thoughts also have the capacity to change the movement and rhythm of the strands just as outside forces influence it. The DNA bends, twists, and compresses like an antenna moving to focus on an incoming signal. During the unwinding movement, fluorescent light is released, exposing more surface area for communication and processing information. As we access new areas of information, reorganization happens in a heartbeat.

"When we think, we set into motion vibrations of a very high degree, but just as real as the vibrations of light, heat, sound, electricity."

— William W. Atkinson[9]

---

[7] Walter Doerfler, "DNA and Its Epigenetic Potential, an Antenna for Cosmic Emissions: Driving Force in Evolution and Energy Transmission?" *Journal of Clinical Epigenetics* 3, no. 1, (2017): doi: 10.21767/2472-1158.100043.

[8] Peter Gariaev, "The Essence of linguistics and wave genetics in theory and practice," *DNA Decipher Journal* 4, no. 1 (2014): 30-38.

[9] William Walker Atkinson, *Thought Vibration, or the Law of Attraction in the Thought World* (Stillwell, KS: Digireads, 2005).

Interestingly, when DNA is put in water and then removed, the information is still present in the water, even with the physical protein structure absent. This is called the *Phantom DNA effect.*[10] This suggests that the DNA structure contains information and that the water is able to hold the pattern of it energetically.

Now is time for us to wash through old holographic patterns and attune our antennae to restoring balance within us.

The idea that we can alter the expression of our genes is called epigenetics, literally "beyond or above the gene," and it has opened the gateway of possibilities for therapeutic treatment.[11] The belief that the DNA is an immovable code and that a genetic predisposition to a disease or condition is an inevitability no longer holds. We are very much responsible for our own health. Only one percent of our genes are fixed, the part that has been recorded through genomic research.[12] The rest, called junk DNA, has switches that we are only recently beginning to understand how to operate. If we acquire an illness, we might be able to find the switch to turn off again those energies which are expressing the disease. For us to visualize ourselves and the DNA molecule as capable of movement and change rather than a coded linear structure helps us realise the possibilities of regeneration.

In my experience, our amazing bodies do not possess any 'junk;' they are beautifully crafted, and it is strange to apply labels that hold us back from realizing optimal health. Learning to communicate with so-called junk DNA is a key for integrative medicine.

---

[10] Peter Gariaev et al, "The Phantom-DNA 'Wave Biocomputer'," Accessed August 29, 2021, https://www.slideshare.net/INVERTONE/the-phantomdna-wave-p-garjajev-v-poponin.

[11] Carlo Ventura, "DNA and Cell Reprogramming via Epigenetic Information Delivered by Magnetic Fields, Sound Vibrations, and Coherent Water," (webinar hosted by HeartMath Institute, April 6, 2013).

[12] Amparo Latorre Castillo, "Why is the percentage of coding DNA so low in the human genome?" Metode.org 2019, Accessed August 29, 2021, https://metode.org/metodes-whys-and-wherefores/why-is-the-percentage-of-coding-dna-so-low-in-the-human-genome.html.

When we tune into this mystery of our continuous creation and can dance and sing with it, we resonate with our Divine Natural Arrangement (DNA). This enfolding and twisting with our own inner orchestra and the symphony of sound and light information in the cosmos, brings forth the changes.

"The beauty of a living thing is not the atoms that go into it, but the way those atoms are put together."

– Carl Sagan

The Importance of Informational Energy to the Body

It is more than chemistry that creates and shapes our body's functions. Chemistry is one measurable system, but there are others that are higher in the hierarchical organization. In 1988, Dr. Michael Gerber suggested that the energy of sound, heat, electromagnetism, and light organizes all living matter.[13] In 1974, Dr. Colin W.F. McClare, an Oxford University biophysicist, discovered that frequencies of vibrating energy are roughly 100 times more efficient in relaying information within a biological system than the more expected physical carriers, such as hormones and neurotransmitters.[14]

Our bodies are electric. It is now accepted that we generate as well as respond to electromagnetic (EM) fields. Remember the static electricity generated from jumping on a trampoline? An alternating current is constantly forming across all our cell membranes. With disease this voltage lowers, and as a result of this change, we have less energy available for the essential

---

[13] Richard Gerber, *Vibrational Medicine: The #1 Handbook of Subtle-Energy Therapies* (Rochester, Vermont: Bear & Co., 1988).

[14] C.W.F. McClare, "Resonance in bioenergetics," *Annals of the New York Academy of Sciences* 227, no. 1 (February 1974): 74-97.

functions of ongoing cellular metabolism. By using a low frequency pulsed electromagnetic field, we can increase this voltage, giving ourselves electrical nutrition to improve cellular efficiency.[15] Injuries are healed faster and more completely by correcting and disrupting unhealthy signals.[16]

Recent research shows that it is possible to measure the differential voltage between the inside and outside of the organelles of cells. Fluorescent DNA molecules are used as the probe and differences can be seen between healthy and unhealthy cells. This is a potential new way to use light and frequency for treatment.[17, 18]

Electromagnetic Frequencies

To detect medical anomalies, we employ many different frequencies of energy, such as MEG (magnetoencephalography), MRI (magnetic resonance imaging), CT (computed tomography) scans, and ultrasound. The body responds to these diagnostic devices giving us visual energetic profiles. However, they are not used as much to treat illness. These invisible forces of different frequencies influence us without direct touch and affect the reality we see and the actions we take. If the medical industry knows that the body responds to these different energies, why have we not gone further and embraced their wider usage for healing? Only those brave enough to face the potential criticism of their peers and the medical establishment are combining scientific knowledge with other paradigms, with some seeing exciting results.

For many years, physiotherapists have used ultrasound machines

---

[15] Jerry L. Tennant MD, *Healing Is Voltage, Healing Eye Diseases* (Self-Published, 2011).

[16] Massimo Fioranelli et al, "DNA waves and their application," *Open Access Macedonian Journal of Medical Sciences* 7, no. 18 (September 11, 2019).

[17] Anand Saminathan et al. "A DNA-based voltmeter for organelles," *Nature nanotechnology* 16, (Jan 2021): 96-103.

[18] Katherine Bourzac, "Lightning Bolts within Cells," *MIT Technology Review*, (December 10, 2007).

to add more energy to the human body. This form of therapy often helps athletes repair from their injuries faster. Shockwave therapy and low-level laser therapy can also help with tissue repair.[19]

"In every culture and in every medical tradition before ours, healing was accomplished by moving energy."

– Albert Szent-Gyorgyi, Biochemist and Nobel Prize Winner.

The Energy of Mitochondria

An organelle is an intracellular structure that has one or more specific jobs to perform in the cell, much like an organ does in the body. Among the more important organelles are mitochondria, which generate most of the energy needed to power the cell's biochemical reactions. It is also believed that it is their informational exchange of energy with the DNA that contributes to the ongoing changes seen in the cells. When a blue-white light is shone upon the cell each mitochondrion has been shown to display the potential energy of a lightning bolt.[20] Imagine and visualize this light energy radiating down and transforming us. In the heart alone there are approximately 5,000 mitochondria per muscle cell, so we have a vast supply of potential energy within us. Mitochondria not only provide us with energy, they are also involved in other critical functions like helping to decide which proteins are made and when to bring about cellular death.

Mitochondria originated from cyanamide bacteria which lived symbiotically within us. Over time they have become inclusions

---

[19] Tomas Nedleka et al, "Comparative effectiveness evaluation of shockwave therapy, steroid injection and radiofrequency medial branch neurotomy," *Neuroendocrinology* Letters 35 no.5 (2014).

[20] Douglas Wallace, KCU University Lecture Series, Kansas City University of Medicine and Biosciences (accessed May 3, 2016, 24:30) YouTube video, 1:14:46, https://www.youtube.com/watch?v=ahlDLjf8c90.

in our cells. These bacteria are still present in plants and the oceans and are highly successful at utilizing light for energy and carbon exchange. Concentra works by harnessing our own electric potential energy through the breath, our thoughts, and communication with the outside environment. Our own rhythm and focus enable the connections.

These tiny yet powerful mitochondria also contain magnetite, a type of iron that responds to the magnetic field of the earth and the moon. There is magnetite present in many areas of our body. It has been suggested from studies of migratory birds that magnetite is responsible for the mechanical 'map' and that the guiding 'compass' is perhaps biochemical and is based on cryptochrome found in the eyes. It is also suggested that magnetite is part of the immune defense system.[21] The soil and air both contain it. The ability for us to sense magnetic fields is termed magnetoreception and may be one of our primal senses.[22] This innate gift is harnessed when learning the art of healing with Concentra. We use it to orient ourselves and to sense the direction of energy flow needed for healing. It is a subject that has fascinated me for a long time, for I am able to feel this in my body, and it has taken me down this avenue of research.

---

[21] Eric Hand, 'The body's hidden compass-what is it and how does it work? ' *Science* Vol 352,6293 (June 2016) 1510-11

[22] Joe Kirschvink, quoted in Kelly Servick, "Humans—like other animals—may sense Earth's magnetic field," *Science News*, (March 18 2019).

The Energy of the Ionosphere

The ionosphere, the layer of the earth's atmosphere that's about 50 to 600 miles above the earth's surface, contains a high concentration of ions and free electrons and generates a sea of frequencies that affect our brainwaves and nervous systems, and therefore our emotions and behaviors. In the gap between the earth's magnetic field and the ionosphere is an electromagnetic standing wave. It was first detected in 1954 by Professor Schumann with an average of 7.83 Hz (cycles per second) and ranging between 3Hz to 60 Hz.[21] In June 2014, the Russian Space Observatory recorded a sudden increase in the frequency of this wave from 8.5Hz to 16.5Hz, with peaks around 30Hz. In January 2017 it spiked at 36Hz. Cosmic phenomena such as solar flares and lightning are known to cause similar fluctuations where a high frequency current is then followed by a low frequency one. The 7.83 frequency lies within the alpha brain wave spectrum, the state of being restfully awake and which has regenerative properties. Theta brainwaves occur between 4-8Hz and are present when we dream, a place for gathering new information and ideas. These extremely low frequencies (ELF) in our environment can be used for healing.

Just as our bodies are sensitive to gravity, they are also sensitive to the earth's solar system's magnetic forces. The EM field that extends from the earth's core to the outer layers of the ionosphere and beyond is intimately connected with the dynamically evolving blueprint of the human body.[23]

---

[23] Rollin McCraty and Annette Deyhle, "The Global Initiative Investigating the Dynamic Relationship between people and The Earth's Energetic Systems," https://www.Heartmath.org (2014).

Living with and Using the Earth's Energy

"The primordial natural energy emanating from the aarth is the ultimate anti-inflammatory and the ultimate anti-aging medicine."

– James Oschman[24]

The Tarahumara, an Indian tribe in Mexico run in bare feet.[25] They eat pinole and chia seeds and are known as the world's greatest distance runners, pushing themselves to the limit. These ultra-athletes run hundreds of miles in the heat without resting and still enjoy the experience. What is it that enables them to achieve such seemingly amazing physical feats? Surely it is not their food source alone. It may be that they intuitively remember how to harness and utilise the free exchange of universal energy and are able to continually fill up their cellular batteries.

Many years ago, I remember reading these profound words by Professor Brian Cox, a popular English astrophysicist: "We are creating disorder in the universe and we borrow back order to heal ourselves." Taken another way, our health and the health of the earth are intimately connected. The foundation stones of this coexistence are cooperation and mutuality—worlds away from division and isolation that exist today. We must be responsible for our part in the relationship we create with the living world.

When my daughter was ill, I tried many things to help the acute and chronic inflammation in her large intestines and so I bought an earthing sheet. This is a sheet with a conductive material such as silver woven into the fabric and connected to the grounding port on your home electrical circuit. This device simulates being in contact with the earth's electromagnetic field whilst asleep,

---

[24] Clinton Ober, Stephen C. Sinatra, and Martin Zucker, *Earthing: The Most Important Health Discovery Ever!* (Nashville, Tennessee: Turner Publishing, 2014).

[25] Christopher McDougall, *Born to Run: A Hidden Tribe, Superathletes, and the Greatest Race the World Has Never Seen* (New York: Vintage, 2011).

infusing it with negatively charged free electrons that are present on the surface of the earth. Your body is encouraged to return to the earth's electric potential and become an extension of the whole field. This has many health benefits including better sleep and reduced inflammation for it helps return the body to balance and homeostasis. Did the earthing sheet help my daughter? It is difficult to say, though she did comment that her sleep felt even more restful than usual. I naturally wanted to try it, and had similarly deep and peaceful sleeps, as well as very vivid dreams.

The Importance of Light Energy for Health

Photons are light particles that exchange energy when they connect with electrons. Every electron has its unique spin, charge, field, and weight. Patterns of light form when large numbers of excited electrons connect.

In 1950, Dr. Fritz-Albert Popp, a research scientist in the field of biophysics, was one of the first people to recognize the importance of light for our health. He discovered that light emissions from the body (biophotons) follow patterns that mimic the world's biorhythms and other sequences. In one of his studies, Popp measured biophoton readings from the hand and forehead of one of his assistants, Sophie Cohen, over the course of nine months. It was discovered that set patterns were present at seven, 14, 32, 80 and 270 days, as well as patterns corresponding to day and night, week, and month cycles.[26] Popp was also interested in whether biophoton activity varied between those who were healthy and those who were sick. He discovered that a body in a state of stress had higher rates of biophoton emission whilst for those with cancer the rate was lower. His work supported his theory that the more coherent the light, the greater the state of health of the individual, and the more diverse the light spectrum, the greater the ability of the person to self-regulate in any given situation.

---

[26] S. Cohen and F. A. Popp, "Biophoton Emission of the Human Body," *Journal of Photochemistry and Photobiology* B: Biology 40, no. 2 (1997): 187–89.

The water in our bodies can absorb light as well as create fluorescence. Professor Gerald Pollack of the University of Washington discovered that the water closest to the membrane of a cell represented a voltage battery and has the capacity to generate light.[27] So we are constantly glowing and not just when we are romantically in love!

I experienced the effect that the absence of light had on my body whilst attending a course on the assemblage point. This position is where our energy field connects with our physical body and to our life force energy. By placing a three-inch piece of black plastic on various places on the front of the body it would block out any light from entering at that spot. When my partner placed the black plastic square on my sternum at the level of my heart, I felt that someone had suddenly cut off my air supply. I was suffocating. It was a horrible moment and I leapt off the couch, dislodging the plastic and knowing I certainly did not want to die yet. The two-way communication system that I had not been aware of previously had been temporarily shut down. We share the same life force as plants, transforming light into energy, and our bodily health and consciousness are the end result of this interaction. This is what I had experienced.

Light has been used for many years to support healing. Ultra-violet light helps with the condition of psoriasis; low-level laser light improves the skin healing of leg ulcers and scar tissue. In the IVF process, the use of blue light shone on the egg and sperm increases the chance of fertilization. Infrared light has been shown to stimulate the inner ear hair cells to improve hearing and balance.[28] In studies with rats who display signs of brain degeneration, light and sound has been used to improve cellular communication.[29] In a 2015 study, light was used for relieving

---

[27] Gerald H. Pollack, *Fourth Phase of Water: Beyond Solid, Liquid, & Vapor* (Seattle: Ebner and Sons, 2013).

[28] Suhrud Rajguru et al, "Infrared photostimulation of the crista ampullaris," *Journal of Physiology* 589 no.6 (2011): 1283-94.

[29] Anthony Martorell et al, "Multi-sensory Gamma Stimulation Ameliorates Alzheimer's-Associated Pathology and Improves Cognition," *Cell* 177, no. 2 (April 2019): 256-271.

pain by activating the natural opioid releasing cells of the body.[30] These experiences show the amazing potential of our innate ability to reduce pain without side effects or foreign particles to digest. The applications of light for the healing process would seem never ending.

The Wonder of Sound for Healing

Our bodies are both containers and amplifiers of sound. In 2002, Scottish physicist James Gimzewski and UCLA graduate student Andrew Pelling observed that oscillating cells made specific audible frequencies. Taking measurements with a highly sensitive, miniature microscope, they observed the motion of different types of cells and recorded their frequencies. When the sound was amplified, they found that cancer cells vibrated at a different frequency than healthy cells.[31] Is this the mechanism by which some dogs can detect unhealthy cells in humans? More research in this exciting new field, known as Synocytology, may some day give us the answer. As we 'listen' to and feel both the obvious and the more subtle sound in the silence, we create new structural patterns and connections. Tuning into these vibrations re-forms the physical body.

Sacred Sound

For millennia, chanting, singing, and rhythm have been an important part of sacred traditions and ceremonies. Buddhist chanting, the drumbeat used by Native American shamans, the connecting measure of the voice and words in Hawaiian 'oli,' the uplifting emotion of Gospel music—the rhythm and vibration of spiritual prayers, music, and verse has a hypnotic effect, connecting us to the essence of nature and spirit. Our cells hold the ancient memories of sounds that have been used for centuries and hearing these can reawaken us to different dimensions of

---

[30] Edward R. Siuda et al, "Spatiotemporal Control of Opioid Signaling and Behaviour," *Neuron* 86 No.4 (2015): 923-935.

[31] Andrew E. Pelling, Sadaf Sehati, et al, "Local nanomechanical motion of the cell wall of Saccharomyces cerevisiae," *Science* 305 No.5867 (August 2004):1147-1150.

ourselves. The experience of sacred sound can dissolve the sense of the individual self, expanding us into the cosmic oneness that holds us all. In that moment we forget ourselves and are changed.

I remember experiencing the transformative effect of sacred sound on a family holiday in Umbria, Italy. One afternoon, on a walk following a delicious bowl of homemade pasta, we stumbled upon an abbey where the inhabitants, six monks, were chanting Gregorian scripture. As I stopped to listen, it was as if time stood still for me. I can remember after the chanting had ended, I was aware of every detail of the surrounding silence, stillness, and beauty. I felt encapsulated and held by the qualities of that energy.

I am lucky enough to have a friend who is a talented sound therapist. I love immersing myself in her 'sound baths,' where tones from drums, gongs, and crystal bowls surround me, awakening and reminding me each time I hear them again of the vast array of human experiences we are able to access. It is a great re-membering and release. I wake up the following morning with aching bones in my legs, as if I have run a marathon. My bones listen to the sounds, responding to the pressure, connecting me to a language that I am learning to decipher. 'Re-membering' is to bring back into wholeness all that we are. Ancient wisdom says that our bones represent the rocks of the earth and all the wisdom and structure that has been present for millennia. When we connect in this way we receive direct information, ideas, and inspiration to help us.

To some animals, sound is more important than light when it comes to perceiving their surroundings. Whales and bats use sound as a form of acoustic vision to navigate the world. They send out sonar waves and 'hear' the way the sound bounces back to them from the surrounding environment.

Infrasound is the name given to low frequency sound below 20Hz. This is lower than the human ear is believed to be able to detect. It is created by the wind, animals, human cells, earthquakes, and many other sources. It can create anxious states in individuals, though often we do not recognize that this may be the cause. (See Schumann frequency pg 63)

It is known that animals including whales and elephants communicate with infrasound, which has the capacity to travel over long distances and around obstacles. Homing pigeons use infrasound to guide their travels, detecting low frequency vibrations from below the earth's surface.[32] Their bodies must hold the memories of the journeys travelled before. Migratory animals recall such information to guide their return passage to their other 'home' for the purpose of breeding or winter feeding.

In 1939, the standard tuning frequency for music was altered from A=432Hz to A=440Hz. It is still the standard pitch today. 432Hz based music is said to have greater therapeutic benefit, for the sound is clearer, more transparent, and the overtones and undertones move more freely. This allows for more individual interpretation and creativity. It is said to be felt more in the body, producing greater relaxation and reducing pain. This frequency vibrates with Phi and the Schuman resonance, the 'fundamental tones of nature.' Exposure to a diverse and natural range of frequencies and overtones helps us to maintain resilience in our system and to return to homeostasis again and again.[33]

Health is a dynamic, homeostatic system fueled by changing shapes, rhythms, and harmonies.

All the cells and organs of our bodies can hear just as our ears do. Sound waves are felt on the skin and absorbed by all the pores of the body and translated throughout the body as information. Many years ago, a specific frequency therapeutic tuning fork was placed over my heart and I immediately burst into tears. I had never experienced this tool before and was certainly not expecting this reaction. I will always remember my spontaneous response.

---

[32] https://cerebrovortex.com/2012/11/08/pigeons-seeing-with-sound-the-perception-of-infrasound/ (July 2020)

[33] Ruth E. Rosenberg, "Perfect Pitch: 432 Hz Music and the Promise of Frequency," *Journal of Popular Music Studies* 33, no. 1 (2021): 137–54.

The Art of Hearing Heartbeats, by Jan-Philipp Sendker, is a beautifully composed novel. It is set in Burma and narrates the tale of a blind girl who could recognize someone approaching by their signature heartbeat. She also knew how the person was feeling that day. It reminds me of this Hawaiian phrase which always captures the attention of my heart. I try to connect with it often:

A ki mele ahua a pu'u

I connect with you in the song of my heart,
the master of my soul.[34]

As you have read, sound waves, whether audible or at very low or high frequencies, can affect us emotionally and physiologically. Some are beneficial and heart opening, such as the tuning fork I had placed on my chest, and can bring us to a place of greater understanding, love, openness, and peace. Other sounds may close us down and affect us negatively. I remember when I was at school, the screech of fingernails pulled down on a blackboard would always cause me to put my fingers in my ears and shut my eyes. Be sure to resonate with vibrations and rhythms that encourage your heart to sing.

---

[34] Harry Uhane Jim and Garnette Arledge, *Wise Secrets of Aloha: Learn and Live the Sacred Art of Lomilomi* (Newburyport, MA: Red Wheel/Weiser, 2007).p 64.

The Amazing Stem Cell

Stem cells are produced by the bone marrow. There are also a large number present in the umbilical cord of a newborn baby. These cells have the ability to become many different kinds of cells in the body. Some are destined to become muscle or nerve cells, whilst others carry the potential to become any kind of new cell. Throughout our lives we continue to circulate stem cells around our body though the number decreases as we age. We know we grow new skin when we cut ourselves, and we can repair and grow new bone after a fracture, but we are constantly regenerating many other tissues and structures on a minute-to-minute basis. Our stomach lining is new every five days; a red blood cell matures in 28 days; and we grow ourselves a new liver in seven years. What a miracle our body is, and sometimes we forget this gift.

in 2013 I attended a lecture in London by Dr. Carlo Ventura on the use of EM fields and low frequency sound waves to selectively stimulate a variety of stem cells. His research is focused on the possibility that by applying the correct field and sound to the stem cells they will differentiate and regenerate existing organs and potentially even grow new ones. At the end of the lecture, he said that his vision was that one day we would all be able to produce our own stem cells for whatever we needed. This idea stirred something deep within me.

A relatively new treatment for arthritic pain involves removing stem cells from fat cells in the body and injecting them into painful joints. The hope is that new cartilage will form avoiding the need for a replacement joint. The body has such an amazing capacity to change and regenerate, and it is an important belief to hold. I marvel at this ability as we become sensitive to our innate ability to heal and 'become anew' leaving the state of health that is no longer helpful.

Developing Our Ability to Sense the Signals Around Us

Our body as the antenna attunes to all we encounter. When we walk into a new environment or meet someone new, we instantly sense information. How we personally notice other energies is unique to us. It's nothing we've seen or heard, but rather an inner knowing, a felt sense. Some may call it intuition. If we feel uneasy in our surroundings, our breathing may get faster, we might talk more rapidly, and our thoughts may lack clarity. I talk in more detail about our physical responses in Chapter 8.

Our unique rhythm with life's sounds and EM patterns governs how we experience the world through our bodies. Studies have shown that our blood pressure changes with the seasons.[35] Blood pressure also has an inherent five-day and 28-day rhythm.[36, 37] We can also experience changes with the cycle of the moon. Many people cannot sleep when there is a full moon. Emergency departments anticipate that they may receive more admissions of patients with mental disorders (lunacy) at the time of the full moon. It is sad that we have divorced ourselves from these natural rhythms that connect and sustain us to the natural world. If we resonate with the cycles of the moon, why not the stars and planets, in fact, with everything that is alive?

Biodynamic gardening looks to the phases of the moon to ensure good harvests and healthy nutritious plants. Many years ago, I became fascinated when reading that cabbage grown biodynamically had greater healing capabilities for cancer than those that were not. This philosophy became popular in

---

[35] Simo Näyhä, "Adjustment of Blood Pressure Data by Season," *Scandinavian Journal of Primary Health Care* 3, no. 2 (1985): 99–105.

[36] Takuya Fujiwara et al., "Seasonal Differences in Diurnal Blood Pressure of Hypertensive Patients Living in a Stable Environmental Temperature.," *Journal of Hypertension* 13, no. 12 Pt 2 (1995): 1747–52.

[37] S Giaconi et al, "Long-term reproducibility and evaluation of seasonal influences on blood pressure monitoring," *Journal of Hypertension* 6, No.4 (Dec 1988): S64-S66.

the west with the anthroposophical movement founded by Rudolph Steiner. Steiner saw a correlation between science, nature, universal laws, and spiritual concerns. Planting seeds, transplanting, and harvesting are all governed by the astrological position and phases of the moon. This concept has also been used by the Hawaiians for centuries. Many believe, and studies show, that planting seeds on a waxing moon and specifically, just before a full moon, can increase the viability of germination due in part to the greater availability of water. Harvesting on a waning moon allows the nutrients and sap to move downwards into the plant and roots, ensuring more vitality and benefit. I talk more about our relationship with the moon and universe in Chapter 7.

In its desire to reach the light a seed germinates by drawing to it the natural forces needed to help it grow.

Our bodies as sensitive barometers are continually recording the inside and outside of our environments. We are affected by many different forms, vibrations and frequencies of energy and as we embrace and become consciously aware of them, we deepen these connections and appreciation for all life. We have evolved with the presence of these energies and so, as we open to living in harmony with them, we reawaken our natural state of wholeness and health.

Thoughts to Germinate

- Our bodies are transducers of energy and are a representation of our perception of and relationship to the world.
- Our bodies are in communication with both visible and invisible light sources.
- Low and high frequency sound affects both our cellular and external behaviors.
- Our bodies resonate with the earth's rhythms, magnetic field, cycles, and seasons.
- The earth responds to our state of being.
- Our DNA responds to thoughts and emotions which defy the conventional laws of physics.
- Our sixth sense is the ability to connect to and navigate with the earth's magnetic field.
- Sound and electromagnetic waves are used to stimulate stem cells.
- 99% or more of our genes have the capability to continually change.

Chapter 4

The Three Brains—Combining Intuition, Wisdom and Logic

"Fuse the powers of the sacred heart with the energies of the body, and you can transform everything."

– Pierre Teilhard de Chardin

Why is it we choose to emphasize the study of the brain and forget the important influence of the heart and gut when looking at ways for improving and maintaining health? The heart has extensive connections with all parts of the body including the 'brains' in the gut and mind. These often forgotten pathways are vital for integrative healing.

The Mind Brain

The brain is what we generally think of when we talk about the mind. We learn that the left brain is the center of logic, thought, and reasoning, while the right brain is the center for our creativity and innovation. The two hemispheres are linked by a bridge called the corpus collosum, which gives us the ability to use both sides together or separately. As we integrate the left and the right, our responses reflect both logical and creative ideas—joined up thinking! Analogical reasoning is our ability to use information from one field of thought to help solve a problem in another area. We can consciously build a map relating all the structures and find a solution. This lateral thinking, looking at the question from another viewpoint, creates the movement to change the relationships within the situation and is used to influence the health and pain of the body. Entering an awake dream state and observing yourself as something different is a good way to access simultaneously logical and intuitive solution finding.

"Work in the invisible world at least as hard as you do in the visible."

– Rumi

Entrepreneurs demonstrate this ability of left and right brain integration. Their enquiring flexible minds operate both in the linear logic of the left hemisphere and the ambiguous, creative freedom of the right. They use both sides to be innovative and experimental, embracing a problem as an opportunity, opening into a moving fluid structural solution. Having a dynamic frame of reference creates energy and power for it opens up greater possibilities.[38]

We are all entrepreneurs, our own creators of the new, willing to experience previously unknown situations and ideas. When engaging with life in this way we experience and will continue to experience vibrant health. Beyond the mind brain, however, we have access to an extensive network of additional information gathering and processing. These are present in connections between the brain, the heart, and the gut. If we use our minds only to conceive from the past, we are closing off that ability to see new perspectives and enjoy new connections. This is neatly summed up by Bradley[38] after reflecting on Einstein's words: "Albert Einstein called the intuitive or metaphoric mind a sacred gift. He added that the rational mind was a faithful servant. It is paradoxical that in the context of modern life we have begun to worship the servant and defile the divine."

[38] R Bradley, "The psychophysiology of entrepreneurial intuition: a quantum holographic theory," Proceedings of the Third AGSE International Entrepreneurship Research Exchange, Auckland, New Zealand (8-10 February 2006).

The Heart Brain

The heart emits an electromagnetic (EM) field, which can be measured up to six meters from the body. It is the body's most powerful and most extensive EM field, 5,000 times greater than the field produced by the brain. Many studies suggest that this heart field acts as a receptor and processor for incoming information.[39] This suggests we can perceive and process data from the geomagnetic systems all around us. We have our own GPS system and as we become familiar with our user manual it helps us navigate the world!

Other research has shown that the heart may be the source of our intuition, perhaps by picking up information from the surrounding energetic field.[40] An experiment by the HeartMath Institute was designed to see how the heart and brain received information and then responded to an event. Candidates were asked to identify happy or angry faces that were displayed at random on the screen. After an initial practice, it was discovered through EEG analysis and skin conductance measurements that the candidates could predict with accuracy the photo about to be displayed up to four to seven seconds before they saw it. It was concluded that the heart received and transmitted the information before the brain, as seeing with the eyes could have played no part in their response.[41]

Through its EM field and through its extensive network of neural connections, the heart communicates a large amount of data to the brain, influencing our decision-making process and helping us integrate our experience of the external world. The heart has been coined a 'little brain' as it has its own nervous system which contains many of the same cells as found in the brain.[42]

---

[39] Rollin McCraty et al, "Shift: at the Frontiers of Consciousness," *HeartMath Institute 5* (2004): 15-19.

[40] Doc Childre, Rollin McCraty, "Science of the Heart," *HeartMath Institute* 1, (2001).

[41] Rollin McCraty et al, "Electrophysiological evidence of intuition: Part 2. A system-wide process?" *Journal Alternative Complement Med* 10, No.2 (2004): 325-336.

[42] J.A. Armour, "The little brain on the heart," *Cleveland Journal of Medicine*, 74 (2007).

"If I create from the heart, nearly everything works;
if from the head, almost nothing."

– Marc Chagall

When we make decisions using only our brain, we are omitting a large wealth of valuable incoming information from other areas. To arrive at the answer which is the most defining and ideal for us at any moment in time requires whole-system communication.

The Bonding of Hearts Between Mother and Infant

I continue to learn so much from young people as their innocent imaginative minds explore and make sense of the world around them. My son asked me how I knew what he wanted when he could not speak to me when he was a baby. How does a mother know?

When a mother and infant are bonding their hearts beat in resonance with open and loving connecting fields. The heart acts as the receiver and transmitter for the infant; the eyes and ears. Holding a baby close to the body where an infant can hear and feel the heart and the touch of the skin is perfect. The baby is fully supported, feeling loved and seen. When a mother is holding the child in the same way, but is on the phone or performing another task, the same depth of bonding is missing, and the child will not settle so well. This heart resonance between mother and child is still present even when the two are not near. The quantum world calls this non-local entanglement. Once you are aware of something there is always a connection. We are the ones to choose how these bonds of connection are formed and function. Giving complete attention to an individual is a powerful gift.

"Attention is the rarest and purest form of generosity."

– Simone Weil

It had puzzled me why a newborn baby has 20/20 vision but is unable to see clearly for about six weeks. Initially, infants begin to see shadows, greys, until finally they recognize and see the beauty of their mother's face, matching feelings with vision. Nature shows us that at that tender age our hearts are more accurate at feeling that expansive, enveloping, caring, and nurturing love than our eyes alone. Maybe this is one of the reasons why there are more nerve impulses ascending from the heart to the brain than descending from the brain to the heart.

The Many Different Roles of the Heart

For me, the subject of the heart is exciting. This one organ has such an essential and varied role in the body. It has many more abilities than acting simply as a pump, as I was taught many years ago. It affects the central nervous system (the spine and brain) as well as the peripheral nervous system and many other body systems. It is also one of our most powerful sources of energy, responsible for how we affect the world around us. As an organ of great mystery, it can reveal and lead us to greater dimensions of our existence.

One of the many ways the heart works with other parts of the body is through the endocrine system, releasing many important hormones and neurotransmitters.

- The heart produces a hormone called atrial natriuretic factor (ANF). This hormone affects the blood vessels, the kidneys, the adrenal glands, and many regions in the brain.
- The heart secretes oxytocin, commonly referred to as the love or bonding hormone and releases it in higher concentration than the brain.[43] It is said that when the level of oxytocin is raised it is difficult to hold a grudge for anyone.

[43] Marc Cantin and Jacques Genest, "The heart as an endocrine gland," *Clinical and Investigative Medicine* 9, No. 4 (1986): 319-327.

- Studies by the HeartMath Institute have shown that with sustained positive emotions, such as gratitude, compassion, and appreciation, the autonomic nervous system resets and energy is radiated out by the heart in the form of a coherent EM field.[44] This is felt by those around us making it easier for others to connect to their hearts too.
- The heart contains specialised cells known as intrinsic cardiac adrenergic (ICA) cells. These release the neurotransmitters noradrenaline and dopamine which are also found in the central nervous system. Dopamine is a hormone which stimulates pleasure and reward.

Get your heart online
and your passions will fly.

The Joy of Heart-and-Brain Communication

When our brains and hearts are in synchrony, our nervous system becomes more balanced, and we are in a state of relaxed alertness and awareness. Our minds are uncluttered and free to let information and emotions come and go freely. In this coherent state we perceive and embody more of the subtleties of life. This could simply be the complexities of a smell, or the nuances felt in your body with a yoga posture, or the ability to release the old and align with new wisdom. We become more deeply aware and sensitive to our true nature and of all that is around us. The HeartMath Institute has undertaken wonderful research over the last 25 years showing the benefits of this resonant state for those suffering from chronic pain, post-traumatic stress syndrome (PTSD), and children with attention deficit disorder (ADHD). Children who have poor concentration skills may be highly sensitive and have less filters to the external world. HeartMath has created a useful feedback tool to help them safely reach this calm and safe place of receptivity and alignment.

---

[44] Rollin McCraty et al, "The effects of emotions on short term heart variability using power spectrum analysis," *American J of Cardiology* 76, no. 14 (1995): 1089-1093.

The human heart may be able to communicate at far greater distances than between a mother and the baby that she holds in her arms. Some research shows that the effect of single, focused events with a global impact may be evidence of resonance at the level of 'global consciousness'. After the tragedy of 9/11 in America, the effect of human global interaction was measured by studying the output from a scientific tool called a random event generator (REG). The graph from the REG displayed greater structure after the tragedy rather than the random variations seen before.[45] Another interesting fact was that the start of the change to greater order was evident a few hours before the first crash. It was as if there was a precognition of this event globally, a united web of consciousness.

A shift in awareness is all it takes to create new fields of vision.

Perceptions of the Heart

Our heart lets us know when we are out of tune with our spiritual responsibilities, life values, and the natural laws of the universe. What do I mean by this? The heart perceives the intangible, formless, timeless, and immeasurable qualities that we feel, yet cannot accurately describe or quantify. It brings to our attention situations or relationships where we are not being true to ourselves. We may notice this inequality in the body as pressure, tension, stress, or other forms of restriction. In a word, we feel disconnected from authenticity and truth. When we are coherent and fully aligned things fall into place. We call this manifestation.

Thus far, the heart is known to influence the body in four ways: through communication via the nervous system, by biochemical and hormonal communication, energetic communication via the EM fields, and through the pulse and rhythm of the muscular contraction of the heart as it pumps the blood.

---

[45] Roger Nelson, "Coherent consciousness and reduced randomness: Correlations on September 11, 2001," *Journal of Scientific Exploration* 16, No. 4 (2002): 549-570.

Our Gut Brain

We all know the phrase 'gut reaction.' We react from our guts spontaneously, without a thought, the survival instinct generated from the unconscious brain. Many times this serves us well but it can also cause problems when we 'shoot from the hip' without dialoguing with other areas of the body; too often we speak and take actions in the heat of the moment. Finding a calm space, spending time in nature, or pausing without reacting and checking on our internal environment will always facilitate a clearer communication, inviting more options for solutions.

Our intestines house trillions of microorganisms, and our own unique community of these organisms is a representation of our interaction with the world. We have more microbes living with us in and on our bodies than we have cells! They originated from the first single celled organisms that inhabited earth. In health, the microorganisms live together symbiotically, for the benefit of each other and for us, contributing to our health and well-being. By maintaining healthy gut microbes, our mood, stress, and inflammation levels are more likely to stay balanced. This 'gut colony' not only manufactures B and K vitamins and houses the vast majority of our happy hormone, serotonin, but it also provides a first-class defense system against unwanted predators that might make us unwell. The healthier and more diverse our gut microorganisms are, the healthier we are.

Along with the bacteria in our gut, the fungi, parasites, viruses, and protozoa in our bodies also respond to physical or mental stress whether real or not. For example, when we live in fear or when we speak unkindly to ourselves, our natural defenses that keep these microbes in balance may become weakened. This feeling of 'other than ourselves' produces a gut response as the microorganisms are moved to behave differently. Our aligned, connected self has just gone off the rails and this creates physical symptoms. If we are sensitive to this change, we may use this information to help us correct our thinking, behaviors, and actions.

A Trilogy – Union of the Three Brains

The integration of these three brains—the head, the heart, and the guts—contributes to a greater sense of self, and an ability to perceive and feel situations from all angles and vantage points and arrive at the most beneficial decisions for all concerned. An excellent book, mBraining, has many helpful exercises to help you tune into these three areas and integrate them.[46]

Many indigenous peoples believe that we have three seats of intelligence that over our lifetime we must get to know intimately. They help us to heal the relationship we have with ourselves and every being in the external world. I have always found it useful to explore others' ideas and so share with you what I have experienced through the Hawaiian perspective.

In the book Wise Secrets of Aloha: Learn and Live the Sacred Art of Lomilomi, the three areas are the Unihipili, Uhane, and Aumakua.

The Unihipili, situated in the lower body, holds the physical and emotional bodies and is the seat of the unconscious mind. By nature, it is innocent and childlike. It responds to symbols, often communicates without words and is quite literal in its thinking. It will avoid conflict at all cost. Traumatic memories become crystallized here, frozen until thawed out. It is from here that our energy and regenerative charge of life is regulated.

The Uhane represents the emotional and mental minds and the spirit of will. The energy body resides here and it is from where the qualities such as imagination, intuition, and psychic abilities are generated. The Uhane extends from the third eye, the pineal gland at the line of the eyebrow down into the heart area. Lono, the Hawaiian God of healing is represented here. Hina, his goddess wife also brings healing gifts. They are a balance of the male and female healing energies.

---

[46] Marvin Oka and Grant Soosalu, *MBraining: "Using Your Multiple Brains to Do Cool Stuff"* (Createspace Independent Pub, 2012).

The Aumākua represents all that is the sacred, our ancestors, the land, the elements of nature and spirit helpers; the benevolent higher forces. It is situated above the crown of the head and extends down into the heart. The higher and parental mind resides here and it is where there is a balance of masculine and female energies. This wise guide gives insights and advice without any intended outcome or direction. The spiritual energy of the Aumākua has been referred to as mana and continually surrounds us. Its manifestations in the physical realm are seen as miracles. This energy operates in the present moment, bringing past and future together.[47]

In the Hawaiian stories it is the God Ku, the architect and builder, who connects these three areas. This is collectively known as the Mauli and represents our essential nature.

So, despite the different names and the many years of passing, those cultures that are more connected to the earth, nature, and to the skies above through the vehicle of their physical bodies, know how to listen to their internal gifts of communication more effectively than most of us today. Through integration of these minds, our subtle senses develop, and we discover patterns and hidden messages in daily occurrences.

The Linking Pathway in the Body

The vagus nerve connects the three brains and is the longest cranial nerve in the body. It is a major player in activating the parasympathetic nervous system (PNS), the calming antidote to the fight or flight response. Initially, when we detect a stressor, something we believe will affect our survival, we become acutely aware of any potential threat. We also may experience physical changes such as a change in our heart rate and breathing rate, a pain in the chest, a feeling of nausea, tiredness, abdominal pain or headaches. With prolonged exposure to stress, other symptoms such as constipation, poor digestion, or repeated

[47] Harry Uhane Jim and Garnette Arledge, *Wise Secrets of Aloha: Learn and Live the Sacred Art of Lomilomi* (Newburyport, MA: Red Wheel/Weiser, 2007).

infections may appear. Over time, we adapt and accept that this heightened fear response is normal for our systems. When these symptoms are present over long periods of time, they may result in inflammatory bowel disorders such as Crohn's and ulcerative colitis; autoimmune conditions such as lupus, Sjogren's syndrome, endometriosis, and rheumatoid arthritis; or diabetes, chronic fatigue, and depression. Alzheimer's, a disease of long-term chronic brain inflammation, is also included. In such instances, the ability of the body to self-regulate and maintain homeostasis has been lost.

A small study at the University of Amsterdam showed that stimulation of the vagus nerve over a four-month period in rheumatoid patients helped to reduce joint inflammation and pain.[48] The Feinstein Institute for Medical Research studies the vagus nerve as a regulator between the nervous and immune systems using bioelectric stimulation. There are many other ways we can help to bring ourselves back into resonance by modulating vagus nerve activity, including specific breathing techniques, using our voices—singing, humming, chanting, or speaking—forest bathing, movement, dance, and balancing our systems with the earth and elements of nature. When we approach all of life as a mindful meditation and prayer, our physiology responds beautifully.

With stimulation of the vagus nerve, oxytocin is released. This hormone, as I mentioned before, is the 'bonding hormone,' which can enhance and deepen the relationship between ourselves and others. This bonding emotion can counteract feelings of loneliness and help us to appreciate the similarities and the differences between people, enhancing social connectivity much akin to the millions of cohabiting happy gut bacteria. We thrive with a greater diversity in our internal community just as we do with having a supporting network of friends and family.[49]

[48] Frieda A. Koopman et al., "Vagus Nerve Stimulation Inhibits Cytokine Production and Attenuates Disease Severity in Rheumatoid Arthritis," *Proceedings of the National Academy of Sciences* 113, no. 29 (July 19, 2016): 8284–89, https://doi.org/10.1073/pnas.1605635113.

[49] Stephen Porges, *The Pocket guide to the Polyvagal theory: The transformative power of feeling safe* (W.W.Norton & Co, 2017).

When the systems of our body start to resonate again, communicating in their natural rhythm, we are able to receive information from the earth, our ancestors, and all of the natural world. As we engage with more heartfelt connections with others, we bring coherence to our internal cellular communication and better health. A greater healthy knowing of the self and the beauty of the cosmos reveals itself to us.

Communication Between Systems

When I count the number of bridges in the human skeleton it is amazing that there are so many strong, structural connections joining the individual parts of our bodies. The lower bridges are in our feet, balancing weight from side to side at the toes and the medial arch supporting our bodies to transfer our movement from front to back. As we move up the body, the pelvis is an obvious huge girdle of strength, holding the legs and spreading the load of our upper skeleton evenly. We have internal bridges in our heart, the arch of the aorta and the many vessels that arc over other structures. Our long bones have thousands of internal intricate osseous bridges that create the optimum alignment for redistributing pressure with every step we take. Our noses, cheekbones and the roof of our mouths come together to form bridges connecting left and right. The optic chiasma is a linking bridge between the left and right eyes and the brain.

As we open our senses to more subtle energies, we will feel our bodies and consciousness strengthening these bridges of connection, allowing us to jump over or reach across these gaps and establish a greater sense of cohesiveness. The way of journeying across safely is by seeing, feeling, and knowing with the heart, blending with the inspirational and thinking mind along with the supporting foundations of the gut. Previous epochs lived primarily with the imbalance of these 'brains' rather than through their collaboration, partnership, and integration. This outdated relationship is no longer sustainable or desirable and inhibits our return to health and community.

We are all searching for the same things: happiness, love, health, belonging, and freedom to be. We first look outside ourselves, seeking rather than being present with what is, until we finally realise these pure intangible essences have been here within us and around us all the time. We can feel them at any time.

When we dare to communicate with our bodies, dialoguing and engaging with our felt sense of pain and unease, the pleasure and freedom we are seeking is there.

"The search for truth,
Where the subtle merges with the gross,
Requires subtle discrimination,
The seat of such discrimination is in
The sky of the heart."[50]

–Swami Chetanananda

[50] Swami Chetanananda, *The Sky of the Heart, Jewels of Wisdom from Nityananda* (Portland, OR: Rudra Press, 1996), 42 : 87.

Thoughts to Germinate

- The heart is an organ of perception.
- The heart gives and receives information from the geomagnetic field of the earth and cosmos.
- The beneficial effect of synchronised human consciousness (togetherness) on the environment.
- The significant influence the vagus nerve has on the mind, alignment, and homeostasis of the physical body.
- Coherent efficiency of the vagus nerve via the autonomic nervous system results in positive hormonal release and has far-reaching health benefits.
- Our immune system is the totality of who we are, and the response can be seen and felt in all areas of the body when activated.
- The immune system is both uniquely personal as well as part of the 'collective human spirit'.
- Communication between the three 'brains' is important for health and happiness.
- Experiencing our body within connects us more intimately with ourselves and others giving space to fully participate in the energetic dance of life.

Part 3

Looking Deeply Within Ourselves

Chapter 5

Exploring Our Finer Senses

"Instinct is something which transcends knowledge. We have, undoubtedly, certain finer fibers that enable us to perceive truths when logical deduction, or any other willful effort of the brain, is futile."

– Nikola Tesla

An integrated, healthy human system is one which fully participates in life, expressing our truly divine nature. Some call this our spiritual essence, encompassing the entirety of our physical, mental, emotional, and dream bodies. We can know ourselves as a single individual unit of the world and as the totality of all we have encountered in life. It is time for us to delve more deeply into the mystery of our personal universe for regenerative healing.

Our Felt Senses

When we open ourselves up to receive healing from this invisible world, we start to develop our more subtle senses. These can also be called 'felt' or 'knowing' senses and they have more structure to them than meets the eyes. The felt sense is our navigation tool, internal compass, GPS, call it what you will. It is the most accurate representation of how we experience the world, and it gives us the power of centering ourselves whenever we use it effectively.

Developing these senses has many benefits. Firstly, as we put our faith in the invisible, the immeasurable, and the unexpected, our perceptions start to expand. Exploring this new awareness of subtle energies leads us to greater contentment, continued creativity, and regenerative zest for life. We learn the ability to easily move between the different facets of ourselves and the challenges and pleasures of life on planet earth. Secondly, it allows us to more fully experience ourselves and our emotions and yet feel no lasting attachment and charge to them. We do not let our feelings obstruct, divide, and polarize us. Yes, we are a part of a chaotic world having experiences in a physical body, but we can learn to center ourselves again and again. As we think more like the natural beings we are, we become informed by nature's wisdom.

A felt sense bears no relationship to our five recognized senses. It is literally 'pre-sense.' Pre-sense comes from the Latin praesentia "to be at hand" and can also mean a divine or spiritual presence or awareness.

A felt sense can be recognized:

- When we feel touched by something without touching it.
- When we feel the warmth of an interaction without the heat.
- When we know the truth about something without any mental thought.
- When we know love without any emotion or words.
- When spontaneous words hold great wisdom.

I started to recognize my felt sense by integrating the feelings and sensations of my own body with the healing spirits of the energies all around. By this method of using my feeling senses and communing with the loving external presence, I now recognize guiding hands that continually help me. This process of integrating the internal and external sensations and energies has helped me to reconnect hidden and divided parts of myself.

Our Sensory Connections With Symbols

Sacred symbols have been used by many traditions over thousands of years. Symbols are resonant structures of connection. Think of and visualize the variety that we see every day: the sacred cross on a church, the illustration of a goddess or other religious icons. Symbols are less explicit than language; when we perceive them, they can affect us unconsciously, and emotions, ideas, and states of being may arise spontaneously. Often, we do not know in words what these signs represent, but they resonate deeply within us, communicating unspoken guidance.

The symbol of a place of worship can often help us connect to our more subtle senses. For example, silence and stillness is often present in a church, synagogue, or temple, where people have prayed regularly. Our bodies resonate with the remembrance of this ancient collective reverence. The more regularly we tune in to it, the more it becomes us.

We receive symbolic images on a daily, hourly, and minute by minute basis and yet we can simply ignore and miss their communication. Why am I staring at that shop sign? What is it reflecting? Why am I singing that song again? What new connections am I making and what old ones am I dropping?

When we hear someone talking with an open, passionate heart grounded in truth we resonate with the message. As we taste and experience goodness in a shared meal, we recognize the symbolism of the surrounding love and shared pleasures. These spontaneous moments of wonder, joy and awe radiate out through the entire body, leaving us lost for words and explanation. They are also symbols of sharing, witnessing, and receiving of the spiritual exchange from the God of our understanding. The extraordinary grace of these moments can bring us to our knees.

We can work with the body as our own unique symbol and vessel of hidden knowledge. As we deliberately turn inwards, we tune into different vibrations and thought patterns. Some of these thought forms may be reflections of the environment around us. Our cells resonate and respond at ever deeper levels the more we recognize ourselves. We let go of the physical and emotional bonds that limit our understanding and open ourselves to other connections. Our bodies respond with subtle or more substantial physical changes which we learn to feel, and soon recognize as symbols of our own wisdom and knowledge.

Developing my Inner Sight

In my life, I receive many guiding clues through communications from animals, flowers, and stars. When they appear in my awareness, I ask myself, what are they teaching me? Then I receive the vibration of the wisdom in my body. For example, if I am about to experience a difficult encounter with someone, I might see three robins in my garden. Because I know they are territorial, I could interpret this as a warning to stay open and not become defensive. When I see or dream of an unusual animal, or a particular flower 'jumps' out of the hedgerows into my sight, I communicate directly with them to discover the medicine behind our meeting. This helps me to be mindful and pay attention to the particular situations that surround me so that I can apply their helpful teachings.

I realized that the changing scenery around me was giving me access to become more aware and present in my unique human experience. For everything around me is my teacher, communicating through one art form or another. To stay awake, observe and be present to what is happening even in the dullest of moments is a skill. Even if your day appears to be a repeat of the day before, it never is. The simple, beautiful, everyday interactions with nature are some of the most delightful and varied experiences of life. There is learning to be had in the smallest detail: watching how a bird twitches its tail; listening to the new chorus of song every day; observing how the birds work together feeding from the seeds left out on the garden table; the march of the ants who toil patiently moving twigs for their new home; the whispering leaves telling of a change in the wind; and the clouds the imminent arrival of a storm. Often, when I am quietly reflecting on life, pausing to contemplate, I am lucky enough to see one or two butterflies appear. Always a good sign!

Here is an example of expanding my felt sense of connection whilst in nature:

"Tap-tap-tap," I heard a woodpecker high in the treetops above. It was a red, black, and white woodpecker hammering out the insects on a chilly, blue-skied winter morning. I listened for a while to the rhythm and vibration of the sound and echo. "Go deep inside yourself," I was told. "You have been wearing a hard hat for too long!"

I followed the orders of my internal voice and investigated. I found myself, not in myself but inside the trunk of the tree. The concentric rings of wood were visible. I could feel the moisture they held, the smell and taste of freshly cut wood. I sensed the fibers splitting as the axe cut through them, yielding to the direction of force applied. I saw the shavings of wood fall to the ground to start a fire burning the wood into a bright flame. The rings that once told the story of the seasons became alive again in the fire.

I noticed the top right side of my head was hurting, as if a penetrating blow was attempting to get my attention. Well, it had! I could feel myself having to brace from falling as I felt a force pushing me to the left. I continued to breathe in and out in this space and gave thanks, forgiving my resistance of the 'hard hat' I was wearing. I focused on my intention to reconnect to that physical place in my body. I listened as I heard the words, "Feel the roots of nature." Spontaneously I dropped down into my body and relaxed, expanding outward.

Putting words to the 'felt sense' of the tapping rhythm helped me to access information from nature that reconnected me to my own center. When I exhaled and felt the roots stabilizing the tree, I felt my own roots reaching down into the earth, stabilizing me, and giving rise to a freeing expansiveness in my head. Though I do not suffer from headaches, I felt a definite physical change. I obviously had a restriction there that I was unaware of until it was gone. I felt freer and lighter, yet straighter and more stable in my body. By listening to the messages our bodies pick up, we can access the healing power of nature around us and use this communication to restore ourselves to balanced flow. The subtleness of these reconnections accesses our ability to weave together the threads of wholeness. There was no need to dwell on my 'hard hat' message, I knew from experience it would limit new emerging possibilities if I continued to wear it. Am I ever stubborn? You bet, and I am now aware of the restrictions it can cause. I am also mindful of developing 'new roots'.

As we begin to experience that every living thing communicates with us, our new awareness propels us to delve deeper into this realm. On another occasion, my help was wanted with an unhealthy-looking plant in the garden. I observed the new top leaves had started to curl in on themselves. I asked the plant what was wrong. After a while I knew that it was positioned at the wrong angle. We found a new space for the pot in the garden. After two weeks the newly emerging leaves were flat and healthy.

On another occasion, the clinic in Kent appeared particularly frenzied. Was it my fragmented energy, or was it something outside that was making me see and feel agitated? Could I re-center myself and help the healing environment of the clinic flourish around me? I remembered patients were arriving at odd times, not many at the correct hour of their morning appointments. There seemed to be some sort of unusual energy surging around the building. Later that morning, a woman fell over outside, blood pouring from her wound. At lunchtime, all the staff commented on these strange happenings and their unfamiliar feelings. In the afternoon we experienced an earthquake. It was only small, but earthquakes are very unusual for this area of Kent.

By being aware of both the inside and outside of our being we experience shifts as they begin to happen. Our bodies are incredibly sensitive instruments, able to translate messages that connect us intimately to the world around us.

The marine park of Kealakekua Bay in Hawai'i has given me many special moments to savour. The presence of nature speaks loud and clear and it focused my desire to listen more to her voice. One morning, as I was swimming in the middle of the bay, I saw a large shoal of fish, a bowl shape at least 30ft wide and 40ft deep. Though the fish were closely packed together, there was a larger central space. I watched for a while and noticed the shape change to that of a horseshoe. I swam into the open space the fish had made and saw a large starfish on the sandy seabed. At first glance it seemed dried and dead. I attempted to swim closer, but perhaps the current had suddenly changed and, try as I might, it was impossible to reach the same spot. Why can't I swim back I asked myself? I heard my inner voice say, that star is dead, there is no need to revisit it again. Receiving these useful messages is a mirror of the world back uniting the unconscious and conscious parts of ourselves. I recalled my contemplations that morning and realized there was indeed no going back.

CASE STUDY
Helen's healing with the buzzards

Helen could not lift her right arm more than 50 degrees without pain after her vigorous gardening and pruning the week before. She was only able to reach her arm behind to touch her leg but reaching further up her spine was impossible. The top of the shoulder was very sensitive to touch.

Helen felt the pain restrict all directions of movement. After asking her to look inside her body, she described an angry trapped feeling that was big and heavy. She became aware of all the other places in her body that were related to this, including under her right rib cage.

After breathing into it, she watched and was able to release the sensations. She felt the place of calm in her body that allowed the shift of awareness. She repeated the process of this internal observation a few times, placing her heart over the heart and giving thanks for the loving, healing connection she could feel taking place.

Within five minutes her pain was 50 percent better,

as she discovered by lifting her arm up. I did not know it, but all the time, Helen had been looking out of my window onto the beautiful field and watching buzzards fly high in the sky. She said that this scene had helped her. She was using the outside to facilitate the physical changes inside.

Helen said she wanted to remember the picture and went home and practiced, visualizing and feeling that same space and scene. After two days she reported to me that her shoulder had full pain-free movement. She confidently told me that she would now be able to use this process for any other pain that arose.

Like Helen, you can train yourself to inhabit your own memory and picture of beauty. Nature in all its glory is freely available 24/7 for you. Make a promise to yourself and share experiences with nature every day. Feel the earth's wisdom—let it spark rejuvenation and help you regain your health and balance.

The Subtle Senses of the Heart

The Hawaiians believe that the heart is the transducer, the encoder, and the amplifier of all that we encounter. What we radiate out depends on how centered we are in the garden of this creator of our understanding.[51] I interpret this to mean we drop our personal and restricting 'stuff' to allow our clear, loving spirit to shine. Tending to our inner garden is essential for the growth of nourishing connections. The heart perceptions are not measurable

[51] David Kaonohiokala Bray and Douglas Low, *The Kahuna Religion of Hawaii* (Borderland Sciences Research Foundation, 1990).

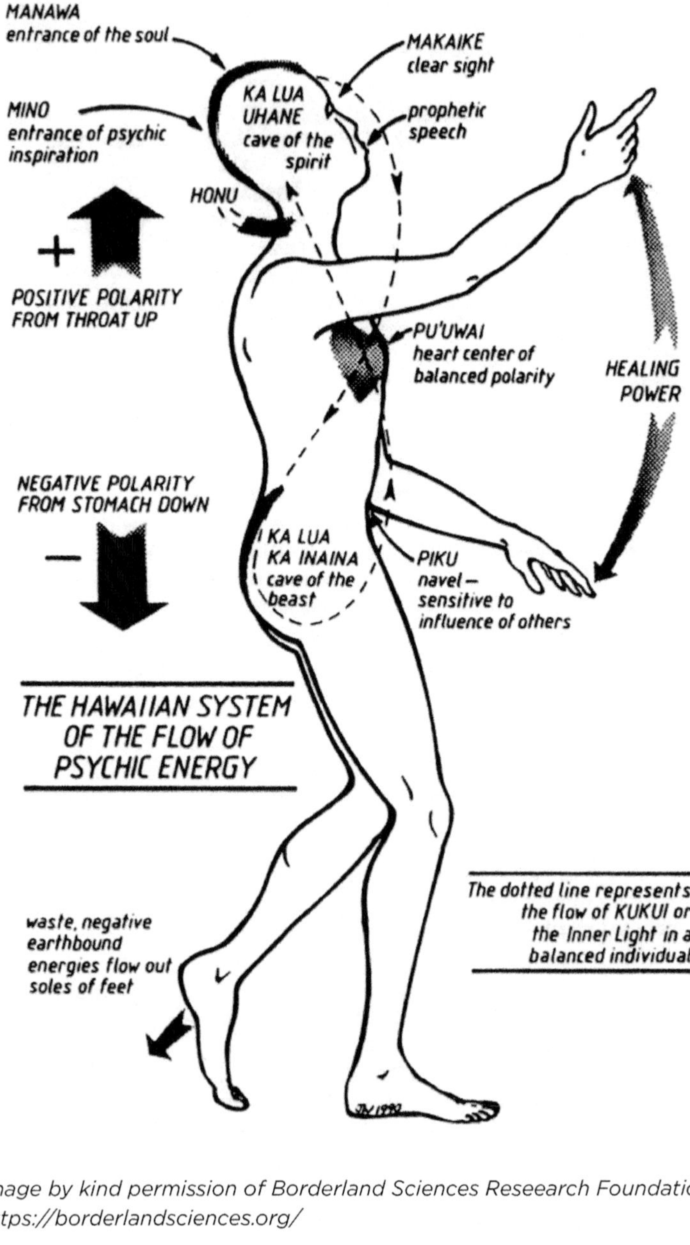

Image by kind permission of Borderland Sciences Reseearch Foundation https://borderlandsciences.org/

either linearly or logically, and they contain neither intensity, labels, judgements, or analyses. The emptied heart is a full one able to freely experience all emotions and it remains freer holding none of them. In this empty balanced system, gratitude, joy, and unconditional love flows.

The Hawaiian story of the bowl of light is an analogy for tending to our 'inner garden.' We are given our physical body as a temple of light, which houses our spirit. When the body feels good so does our spirit and vice versa. The Hawaiian myths tell us that we are all born with the ability to swim with the turtles and dolphins and slide down the colors of rainbows. We all possess magical abilities, and our inner child remembers this if we ask. Over the years, we unconsciously pick up heavy stones along our paths filling our bowls of light. We forget what we are capable of and our light dims. We start to suffer physically. Our piko, our belly buttons, the connection through the umbilical cord to the womb of our birth Mother and to the Earth and to the source of all creation, is disrupted and we become sick. The spiritual energy, or 'mana,' is disturbed. The beauty for us all in this Hawaiian story is that at any time we can turn the bowl over and empty out the stones and reconnect to the true source of light. We begin with Ho'oku'u, releasing the old and starting anew, refilling our temple with the light and language of love—aloha. The skill to learn is to keep the light shining so that stones pass through us, rarely sticking to the sides. We can learn to make wiser choices from listening to the union of our whole being, the three brains.

In the Hawaiian language, our health and well-being is called our mauli ola. The way we think, feel, and experience the events and people around us determines how much light we experience flowing in our inner being and is a reflection of the vitality and joy we share with others. This natural accumulation of light energy is an innate communication system within each of us and is both dynamic and self-organising.

"You can't reason with your heart; it has its own laws, and thumps about things which the intellect scorns."

– Mark Twain

We cannot measure truth, pain, beauty, love, joy, awe, wonder, gratitude, compassion, and wisdom and yet they are priceless and timeless. How do we know what these are? As infants they are our nature. As we grow, we experience these values through our bodies and finally through recognition by words. Our body is neuroplastic which means it is able to change the way it responds to stimuli. New pathways need only a spark of new energy and intention for the connections to form. Health and wellness pathways are enhanced more rapidly when we engage playfully, having fun.

Our felt sense of being touched, moved, and connected with the essence of another forges this neuroplastic capability. This felt sense is part of the experience of giving and receiving human warmth, closeness, and connection. In the same way, we can become touched by an event, or get in touch with how to follow a dance step. We do this subconsciously, without the use of our mental abilities. Did you know that if you watch someone exercising, your muscles believe they are actually joining in, and they can strengthen by 20 percent without physically moving! We are mirroring and creating that environment within us by paying attention. Our dynamic self-organizing system picks up information for us before we are aware of it.

Our Sense of the Language of Invisible Energy

I was curious how it was possible that my four-year-old son could run around continuously with so much energy, so I asked him: "What do you do when you run out of energy?" He replied: "I just rest on the green grass until I feel full up again." My interpretation of his words was that he was still connected to nature's available free energy that supplies healing and regeneration. It was so easy and natural for him. This message stayed with me. What was he reminding me of that I had forgotten? Did he see the energy being given off by the grass? Did he feel it? Did he absorb the green, feel the colour? Or did he listen to the invitation from the earth as a friend? At that time, I did not remember this language of communication.

"A sight, an emotion, creates this wave in the mind, long before it makes words to fit it."

– Virginia Woolf

Is it that we as adults never knew the right language, or did not know how to use it? Did we just adopt another language forgetting the original? It is time for us to access all our 'sense tools' and harmonize these communications coherently.

> *As the mental chatter becomes quiet and heart and mind unite, we are connected as we once were to the point of creation.*

When we watch children playing hide and seek it is clearly a very different experience than what adults experience when they 'play' this game. I remember being fascinated seeing young children sit with their eyes covered in the middle of a room and shout, "I'm ready, find me." In their minds, if they can't see us, we can't see them. They are able to become invisible, camouflaged as part of the furniture, merging themselves with what is around them at the time. They can easily move between the two realities, for they are part of both the material world and the invisible spiritual realms.

My son grew up loving soccer. It seemed like a meditation for him, being 'in the zone,' connected to his developing skills and yet part of a larger team of players. I remember watching him in one particular match when he was about 15 years old. In the second half he had been taken off the pitch. I had seen how he was a key player that game, working the center field. He had an uncanny knack for uniting the team to play well together. For a moment I was worried that the players would become scattered and lose focus. I continued to watch the match as did my son from the sideline. I observed and felt his presence in the middle of the pitch even though he was observing from afar. He had not separated from his love of participation with the team. I relaxed and watched our team to victory. His continued connection without his physical presence reinforced to me the belief that we participate in events he energies and thoughts we give to them. I wanted to discover my own key to this creative ability to participate in the most optimal way at any moment. It reminded me of the phantom DNA effect where even on removal of the physical structure the informational energy is still present.[52]

I loved helping children in the clinic as they taught me many things. They had their own unique way of letting go of stress and moving past their restrictive boundaries. They were often unable to say what the problem was exactly, or sometimes would just recount what their parents had interpreted for them. The parents would cite the issues as bullying, not wanting to go to school, bed wetting, poor concentration, and lack of confidence. It was important for me to give the children space to find their own answers and let go of absorbed ideas from others around—including me with my own agenda. The most common communication would be, "I just don't feel like myself" so I would ask, what would help them feel like themselves again. From this starting point, they could journey into themselves, pick up balloons, bows and arrows, climb trees, swim in the sea, wriggle around on the couch, until they 'found themselves' again. Their finishing point was always obvious. They knew they were healed, reconnected to the part they had unconsciously known was hidden. Many times, few words had been spoken. Feeling 'special,' they would relax into themselves and often would not want to get up off the couch. Others would fall deeply asleep. Abdominal pain, headaches, recurrent neck and back pain, in fact, any symptom without a specific medical cause, would be changed. Loving compassion is a wonderful healing energy.

[52] Peter Gariaev et al, "The Phantom-DNA Wave Biocomputer," Institute Control of Sciences, Moscow, accessed September 1, 2021, https://www.slideshare.net/INVERTONE/the-phantomdna-wave-p-garjajev-v-poponin,.

CASE STUDY
Georgie's miserable birthday celebrations

Every year on her cousin's birthday Georgie was sick. She was unable to eat for five days. Spots appeared on her face and she had pain at the bottom of her breastbone. It happened like this on her own birthday too. She had undergone many examinations to ascertain what the problem was, but to no avail. She was now 18 years old.

We started the session. Georgie softly focused and felt into the discomfort of each of her symptoms. She remembered that when she was six years old, she was sick and could not go to a birthday party that she had been looking forward to. She saw herself as feeling separated, fed up and left out of all the fun. Using Concentra, she felt for the answer outside of herself and brought it to her being. After a while she was able to balance it in all directions and accepting the feeling of the new experience.

Following this healing connection, Georgie was able to enjoy birthdays again with the new freedom to believe that she was allowed to have fun and join in. Her sense of isolation and 'undigested anger' had dissipated.

Children love to pretend to be famous. They idolize pop stars, football players and multi-million-pound businessmen. What is it that they see in them and not in themselves? For some it may be the money, for others the excitement of being famous, or perhaps they see huge creativity. We all want to good at something, to be special. It can be as simple as always knowing what to say in a crisis, being able to feed our families nutritious food, or coming up with working solutions for challenging situations. We may desire to be a famous explorer and discover a new world or create a new invention. This playground of creativity is a fundamental part of our being. We put aside our creative space when we tell ourselves we are not good enough or when we listen only to others. We dumb down of our innate ability to be and to feel anything we choose. We are this power of regeneration. By developing our senses in the imagined world, we come to know our unique gifts and talents.

We often hear about an individual's gifts when we attend his or her funeral. What are we really interested in hearing? Are we only interested in the astute business acumen of the deceased, or also the ability she or he had to turn people's lives around with a little laughter, kind words of support, and advice over a shared meal? We are perhaps searching for our own values, happiness, and contributions to life on earth.

"The human race has only one really effective weapon and that is laughter."

– Mark Twain

The Power of Laughter

Children laugh spontaneously and more often than adults. Laughter creates a space of sharing and connection. It is contagious and affects all those who hear it, nourishing spirits and healing broken bodies. Laughter reduces pain and disease, boosting the immune system by raising levels of our immune protector cells. As we breathe more deeply, our face and abdominal muscles receive a work-out and our organs are tickled. If a joke is told or a situation is humorous, laughter produces a whole brain response. We are stopped from analytical thinking and we relax. The same delta brain waves that are produced during deep sleep promoting healing and regeneration are also produced during laughter. Babies in the first year of life display high levels of delta waves, both when asleep and awake. Interestingly, at the time of death, delta waves predominate.

Laughing with my mother helped her to dispel her worry over her future hip replacement. She described the forthcoming event as a maelstrom, weighing her down taking away her energy. A friend had reminded her that her operation was on Ascension Day which she thought was a little worrying but also quite funny. I asked my mother what she would feel like without any worries. "Not at all like myself," she replied, "the hospital is unfamiliar and ... heavens above, I would not know what to think about." We both laughed for a good while as she embodied heaven on earth without having to ascend and leave earth. "That sounds good," she said. "I will go with that one." The maelstrom of heavy energy lifted.

Laughing for 15 minutes has the relaxing effect equivalent to eight hours of meditation. It is a great medicine and is free and available every minute of the day. The ancient Greeks believed that humor was a virtue and Plato advocated its use as a healing practice. The purpose of the blood moving around the body as in a belly laugh was to collect repressed and unloved emotions.[53]

---

[53] Brian Luke Seeward, *Managing Stress: Principles and Strategies for Health and Wellbeing* (Burlington, MA: Jones and Bartlett Publishers, 2008).

The Invisible Realms of Creativity

Recognizing our finer senses helps us to play and design our world. When we pause and give ourselves the time to play as children do, we co-create with the dynamic patterns and language of the universe. I remember as a child the excitement at discovering my creation when I joined the numbered dots together. This anticipation of an emerging image always stayed with me. Sometimes, I would miss the arm, or draw the legs together, but generally my artwork did resemble the intended original, it just had my novel touch. (My mother kept my little creations!) I was not so keen on coloring books. Using one color on large sections of the person or object seemed less creative and not as enjoyable, and my lack of patience often got the best of me. It was as if someone had already done half of the creating for me. Detailed, multifaceted shapes were much more appealing to me: cubes, circles, hexagrams and stars. I much preferred this kind of coloring book. Even though they appeared to be all the same, you could join the same shapes together, color them differently each time, creating a regularity that was appealing, interesting and yet always different. Patterns would form within the patterns and new shapes would emerge the more I focused on the way they connected. Each time I drew and colored I was creating a joy-filled space of exploration and wonder.

The world does have a working pattern we are familiar with, and we do know how to dance and weave with it. During difficult times it may be necessary to tear up the paper and cross out the pattern, pick a new color and alter the original design, all the while persistently birthing new connections. All challenges help us to seed new creative pathways.

Let's take the analogy of a recipe. The word originates from the French, meaning 'prescription.' Do we ever create the same taste, smell, and experience from the same ingredients? I love to cook. I keep my favorite recipes in a book to use when the mood takes me, or when I'm presented with a selection of the right ingredients. Despite following the same instructions each time, the dish never tastes the same. Some bemoan this and see the variation as a disappointment, wanting the same tasty delight. I relish the new experiences, unless they are complete disasters, of course. I want everyone I cook for to feel nourished. I especially try to remember to refrain from adding extra chili, for I know some of my guests dislike the heat! I am ever eager for new tastes of life that touch my palate, although this can sometimes misguide me into desiring more and more. Whilst in Bhutan and choosing from the dinner menu I was reminded of other life choices. After reading the menu I asked Lama Nyima Tsering whether he preferred Indian or Bhutanese food. His simple, yet profound reply, was that he was content with either.

Creation Mythology

Through the ages, peoples have sought to find answers for our creative existence. Myths, stories, and the science of studying the universe (cosmology) recount similar themes throughout the nations of the world. It is useful for us to look more closely at the cycle of birth and death and the interplay with the elements of nature through the Creation Goddesses.

Neith is an ancient goddess of weaving and war and was thought to be the first and prime creator of the world. The original Egyptian meaning of Neith is 'Divine Mother.' This goddess is the container for the seeds of creation, and she is able to give birth, creating parthenogenetically, without a partner. She is a water goddess and by her giving birth as she does, she is an 'Opener of the way' for us all.[54]

From the Australian aboriginal creation story there is the image of Yirgana, their creation mother who is able to create from every part of her body.[55] I love this image of creation occurring through every pore, and often meditate on it.

---

[54] "Neith," Ancient Egypt Online, accessed September 1, 2021, https://ancientegyptonline.co.uk/neith/

[55] Inés Domingo Sanz, Sally May, and Claire Smith, "Communicating through Rock Art: An Ethnoarchaeological Perspective," 2016, accessed September 1, 2021, https://doi.org/10.13140/RG.2.1.4539.6244.

In Hawaiian mythology, Haumea is the fertile creative goddess of the sacred earth and is known as the ancestress of the Hawaiian people. "She is venerated as the spiritual essence of that ageless womb out of which life is produced in changing forms."[56]

The Imaginal World of Dreaming

"My brain is only a receiver, in the Universe there is a core from which we obtain knowledge, strength and inspiration."

– Nikola Tesla [57]

We can all use our imagination and enter a dream state, whether awake in the day or sleeping at night. But how many of us use this natural ability of direct communication and revelation to heal? The process of dreaming not only centers and stabilizes us but expands our connections to greater sources of wisdom. It is a state of mind which results in the conception of an idea, an organization of energy, without, or before its manifestation in reality. There is no better time than now for us all to utilize this process for inquiry and health, not only for ourselves, but for our families and the rest of the living world. Once we put our trust in the art of dreaming, we can experience physical healing, insights, and guidance in our lives. Dreams can be thought of as virtual reality reprogramming models for our immune systems.

The communication given in dreams is often relayed through metaphors based on memories and in such a way that we can access abstract knowledge through pathways that have unique meaning for us. These perceptions present themselves in relation to stories playing in our current or future lives and help us to generate newly structured thoughts that we can act upon. In this realm of virtual reality, we see new openings, doorways, and

---

[56] Martha Beckwith, *Hawaiian Mythology* (Honolulu: University of Hawaii Press, 1986).

[57] Nikola Tesla, *My Inventions: The Autobiography of Nikola Tesla* (Eastford, CT: Martino Fine Books, 1963).

possibilities to investigate. I have found that for me, dreaming on an airplane or in nature are easy places to let go and enter this creative space. Dreaming in the day or conscious dreaming at night is a skill to practice and is one of my favorite ways of helping myself. It is possible to see ourselves healthy and whole in a dream state. There are many books on dreaming to help us navigate life with wisdom. I enjoy the information shared by Daniel Stone, Robert Moss, and Sandra Ingerman, and more recently Sergio Magaña.

We can take inspiration from one of our greatest inventors, Nikola Tesla, as he spent the first 17 years of his life dreaming before taking action and transforming his revelations into revolutionary working models.

CASE STUDY
Joanna dreams of bridges

"I would like to feel less unstable on my feet and feel that my swallowing and breathing was easier," Joanna requested. "It is sometimes hard to take a deep breath and feels like I am choking." Joanna had suffered a stroke two years earlier that had affected this ability.

I asked Joanna to feel that area in her body. English was not her first language, and I could sense she was a little reluctant to dialogue with me. I asked her to step through the doorway that would find the answers she was looking for.

"I see a bridge quite far away." She was puzzled. Many people were crossing it. I asked if she wanted to get closer to see it. "Yes," she said. "It is safe, and people are going in both directions. There was

a long silence and then she started to cough, and we both experienced the stale air that suddenly appeared in the room.

"That's good letting go of that," I commented. She agreed and went back to studying the bridge and breathing the cleaner air. I continued with the touch techniques on her body helping the energy to flow up and down and to the left and right. There was an area on her left leg that needed deeper work, so I massaged the area in order to free the tight tissues.

After about ten minutes I asked, "Do you want to cross the bridge?"

"No," she replied.

The following night Joanna dreamt about the time she had fallen from a horse when following her friend over a bridge. After the event she had fallen out with her friend about what had occurred.

In an example of synchrony, before the next session the very same friend decided to plan a visit. This would not be a simple drop-in visit, for she lived a six-hour plane journey away.

Finally, the bridge had been crossed. In her dream, Joanna had called to herself what she needed to heal all aspects of the "bridge episode" and had crossed over it. This was the start of her new relationship with this event and her friend. The bridge helped her to access the physical healing she required for her desire to breathe and swallow with greater ease.

When I was a young child, I had a recurring dream, especially when I had a fever. I was trying to catch a ball of wool that was rolling down a dark hole faster and faster and was unwinding as it went. I could not catch it to roll it up again no matter how much I tried. This upset me and made me very scared. I had no idea why I needed to reach the end of it and make a neat ball. More recently, I experienced the same dream in slow motion. I could still see the thread rolling away from me in the dark, but it was easier to see, and the ball was not so far away from me. I was able to watch without fear for I did not need to stop it and rewind it all. I saw the other end of it, close to me on my left, golden light illuminated it. It felt like a remembering of the beginning and the end of a continuous cycle, and I was the journey in between. When I reflected on it, I could not decide which was really the end and which was the beginning.

Beyond Words - Expanding Our Ability to Listen, Hear, and Speak

"Words, English words, are full of echoes, of memories, of associations."

—Virginia Woolf

Words are clearly defined in dictionaries, but these definitions often do not capture the subtleties of our full experience of their meaning. We create our own relationship to words, which is important to remember. Words are like atoms orbiting with potential energy and wisdom. Ask and pray for guidance before speaking, for every communication is important.

Our inner voices talk to us in a variety of ways, sometimes lovingly, and for me, often critically. Unkind words create an atmosphere of pressure inside our bodies which leads us away from our central compass point of happiness, clarity, and peace.

We become separated from the loving presence that is our true self and unconsciously we acknowledge this. Irritation, anger, or overwhelm may consume us, or we may project hurtful words at others. Perhaps if we speak unkindly to ourselves it may invite the same response from others. When we feel worthy of being ourselves and safe with our own sovereignty, our words become fewer and wiser, as we become more openly connected through the silence of our whole being. Listening attentively leads to hearing. The more open the receiving channels, the louder the sound.

The space of silence embracing the echo is as profound as the words.

Bringing Awareness to Our Experiences

Will you follow all the words of advice I choose to give you? Far better for you to delve into the echo and choose from your own vocabulary of word atoms, hearing the form they create. Your story may contain the same words as others, but the meaning is personal, and your interpretation is far better than I or anyone else can give to you. I believe that words create in each of us a unique experience, analogous to the individual feeling of pain.

You do not know my mind; you only have a glimpse at it when I do not know it myself.

Words of poetry or the lyrics in songs generate spontaneous feelings and emotions. We become inspired by the dream—a picture painted in words. This poem reminds us of the juxtaposition of looking and seeking and knowing it is already there.

Are you looking for me?

Are you looking for me? I am in the next seat.
My shoulder is against yours.
you will not find me in the stupas, not in Indian shrine
rooms, nor in synagogues, nor in cathedrals:
not in masses, nor kirtans, not in legs winding
around your own neck, nor in eating nothing but vegetables.

When you really look for me, you will see me instantly -
you will find me in the tiniest house of time.

Kabir says: Student, tell me, what is God?
He is the breath inside the breath.[58]

We often use metaphors to describe pain. All metaphors are transformational phrases and we can use them creatively to change how we experience a problem. The best metaphors are the ones we spontaneously come out with. These are some I have heard:

- "My knee is a pile of rocks just about to collapse in a heap."
- "I was heartbroken, sick to my stomach when I found out."
- "My lungs are straining to give me enough air."

We are inner dialoguing with ourselves at an unconscious level all the time and when we are mindful, an invaluable road map is revealed to us. When we become aware of how we view ourselves through metaphors, we may discover that by reframing these metaphors we can establish a more healing, regenerative relationship with ourselves. A newly framed metaphor might sound like this:

---

[58] Kabir, The Poetry of Kabir: *"All know that the drop merges into the ocean, but few know that the ocean merges into the drop"* (Portable Poetry, 2014).

- "My knee feels as solid as a rock now."
- "My heart is fragile, but I see it mending."
- "I smell the freshness of the air now."

Other metaphors I have witnessed before physical changes are experienced include:

- "I open one door of the house and let the waters flood in, and then open anther door and I see them flow out."
- "Every time I let go on the toilet, they flush away, faraway."
- "My tummy hurts, I want to be able to combust my food better."

CASE STUDY
My understanding metaphor with Flora

The body can be quite literal sometimes. I love the sense of fun and ingenuity it brings to each healing journey. My friend Flora and I like to take regular walks along the coastline looking out across the sea towards France.

On one such walk, I noticed Flora was limping. She was not able to stand fully upright nor stride out as far and as comfortably as she wanted to. We discussed the problem as we walked, and eventually Flora began to connect more fully to the discomfort in her hip and pelvis and to the felt sense of her "under-standing."

By staying present with the discomfort and using her breath to circle the energy up and around her body, Flora experienced a different movement and flow.

We looked at the many blue hues of the sea, the birds gliding above the water and felt the weak sun blown away by the strong south-easterly wind. The witnessing we both gave and received for the other was the gifting of space for healing. No further words were necessary, for the invisible fields of love and intention were sufficient.

Flora was also helping me during our talk. Sometimes I have difficulty in structuring what I am experiencing, but if someone asks me a question, I am often more able to transform my felt sense into words, understanding it myself on another level. Then this will often bring about changes physically. The new idea I understood with Flora was that perception is the energetic blueprint the physical body needs to change structurally.

The next time I saw Flora she told me that at her next yoga session her hip was more flexible, and she could walk further than had been possible in months. I too had my own new understandings of how to teach others.

The art of exploring and integrating sensory experiences is natural in infants. We are not aware we have two arms until we investigate them. We become aware of our toes and fingers by playing with them. Once we accept and integrate their existence, we do not need to fixate on them. Somewhere along the way we forget our limitless awareness and begin to rely on limited, restricted sensations and perceptions. We hold on to the awareness of pain, giving it form. In one sense, the more we move beyond the feeling in our bodies the more awareness we have. But the art is in feeling the sensations and pain first, acknowledging them, and then allowing a new awareness to arise.

Everything we experience is relative to us. When emotions and sensations are no longer a cause producing an effect, then they can pass through unheeded. It is simply an awareness. If we release the emotion within 90 seconds it leaves us with an open fresh empty system once again.

I recognized this same phenomenon of emotional attachment and release as I was leaving the theater in London after attending a Christmas pantomime. There was that wonderful feeling of breathing in the cold air, the dazzle of the bright lights outside the theatre, and the sense of contentment after shouting at the villain with the rest of the audience so that the story would have a happy ending. The emotional experience of being caught up in the plot of the play dissolved into laughter and peace.

We all have the beautiful fairy godmother in us, bringing us joy and helping us when we need, and we also have the wicked stepmother who appears now and again to show us another side of our nature. If the other had no part, we would never recognize the value of each. There would be no story to tell, no happy ending. Peter Pan with his eternal youth, drive and wisdom, and the mean Captain Hook bringing out the free spirit in us all—both have their part to play.

Our encounters in the world are showing us how to love, how to play out our own story. If we exclude any of the characters, or only acknowledge the 'good' ones, will our story seem real or worth reading or experiencing? We must know our own minds as we know characters in our favorite book; not only the one that tells me I am not good enough, the one that says don't write your book today, go and meet a friend instead; not only the one that only analyses and then pretends it knows what it is talking about; not only the one that the medical profession measures by attaching electrodes to our heads.

There is another mind, a presence of being that can look and feel without judgement, impartial, but present with what is occurring. This mind is curious and open to the unknown, at ease in uncomfortable situations. This mind has a different quality of knowing, which relies on spontaneous insights. We are unable to truly hear it if we are not present with what is arising in front of us. This mind is available to us all whenever we want it.

Through a deepening inner dialogue with ourselves we grow into and around ourselves.

It is easy to go along with someone else's idea: it seems right not to rock the boat; it has always been done that way; it is morally and politically correct in the society we have built. But what is your truth? Do you see it another way? Maybe others feel the same and are too scared or shy to speak. In a meeting, you go along with the consensus of opinion for fear of losing your job, being the 'bad guy,' or looking stupid for speaking out. But being polite can muffle or completely hide our own voice. On the other hand, being autocratic, a bull in a china shop, angry and provocative, is rarely effective either. Engaging with the diversity the world offers and believing the insights that your subtle senses illuminate for you, will bring respect and the desired outcome for all. Authentic, loving presence will always create new bonds and can melt any problem that ever existed. To enter into any worthwhile relationship requires listening to other people's points of view as if they were your own and recognizing the truth of the two.

Finding Comfort in Our Sense of Place

A client once told me she had come to the conclusion that she did not fit in. She felt lonely, at a loss as to how to live her life. She was reflecting on how intimately she related to the relationships in her life at present. "What a wonderful realization to come to," I replied. "There is nothing for you to fit into, you are unique and as such there is no template. As you fit into yourself you fit in everywhere."

Years earlier I had helped another client heal her facial pain.

CASE STUDY
June felt her face does not fit

June came to me and said: "I have had this pain on the left side of my face for over 18 months and nothing makes it better. Sometimes I get headaches with it, too, and it is painful to brush my hair. The neurologist says I have trigeminal neuralgia and suggests I take medication, but it makes me feel very woozy. Do you have another alternative way to help me?"

I asked June to dialogue with the areas affected and start up a healing relationship with them. She raised her left hand to her face. "If I touch it, I feel scared but then, as I do it more, it starts to feel like my skin wants it. I feel it is soothing it and it is getting a little warmer."

As she continued, I saw her breathing slow down, the worried look on her face relax, and her eyes soften. She was experiencing something different.

After a minute or so June said: "I remember when I came back from the operating theatre to the ward after a minor surgery. I was met by a nurse. I heard her say: 'I do not like the look of her, she is not coming onto my ward.' The nurse had wanted June to spend more time in the observation room. In her confused state June had felt a separation, of not being right or fitting in and thought she was very ill. These emotions and beliefs had affected her face.

June continued: "My daughter who lives in Canada gave me a surprise visit a few months ago. I remember opening the door and seeing her and she gave me a hug saying how well I looked. I still recall my surprise both at seeing her and her comment." Her daughter had spoken the exact opposite words from what the nurse had said which was the healing remedy June needed to feel accepted again.

After our session, June's headaches disappeared, as did the face pain and numbness over a couple of weeks. The remaining neck ache was alleviated with soft tissue work.

"Courage is what love looks like when tested by the simple everyday necessities of being alive."

– David Whyte

When we develop our subtle senses, we feel a deeper sense of belonging which helps us to take greater risks, venture into new territory, and try new things with less hesitation. Courage is this measure of our desire to become aware, our desire to participate with life, with our families and community, and with a beloved other. We do not need to go anywhere or do anything extraordinary except to make conscious all that enters our field of awareness: to be consistent, persistent, and to continue to feel and participate even when experiencing our own vulnerability.

> *"We can judge our progress by the courage of our questions and the depth of our answers, our willingness to embrace what is true rather than what feels good."*
>
> –Carl Sagan

I still experience some fear embracing my own demons and facing the unknown, and yet, by harnessing my courageous heart and human spirit and with the help of friends and family, my fire still burns brightly. I now appreciate the benefit of experiencing fully the energy of emotions and then being able to release them, no longer anxious that they will overwhelm me. The feeling of peace, stillness and silence which arises is a simple, wordless understanding. Believe in yourself, use your own GPS, listen to the wisdom within, and learn to read the language of energy. I am eternally grateful for this ability to connect to my own dreamtime, my master, and the song lines of the earth's calling.[59]

While I was working with a young man, he wrote a beautiful poem, titled 'Two Birds, One Stone' that demonstrates the magic of internal reflection and creativity I have talked about here in this chapter. I include it here in this book. It shows how we can heal ourselves by connecting with the subtler senses of our being brought to us by the external world.

---

[59] Song lines are maps of the land chanted and dreamed by the Aboriginals of Australia. Each clan participates in the songs giving thanks for the land that they are travelling through and to. Across the land the song lines join, sounding the watering holes and hunting grounds. They are believed to be based upon information from the stars.

Two Birds, One Stone

Knowledge, strength, insecurity
Playing up to the camera
playing down in isolation

Has everything he wants
But little of what he needs

Exuberant bravado
and self-indulged egos
mask the frail child within

Forever scared to show himself
For his self-created reality
is not where he wishes to be

No single approach can provide all the solutions to the release of pain. There is never just one right way. Engaging with the realities of a situation from as many perspectives as possible brings wisdom, vulnerability, humility, and beauty and a greater chance of healing outcomes. When we allow our spirit to speak, the silence and essence of that shared breath brings greater understanding and healing connections. As our own spheres intimately touch with others, we joyfully resonate with the sound of tension releasing; the unifying language of energy.

"All know that the drop merges into the ocean,
but few know that the ocean merges into the drop."

– Kabir

Thoughts to Germinate

- New perceptions await us when we drop our inner dialogue and attention to past experience.
- We create clarity and freedom when we engage with new shapes and structures of connection.
- Our knowing hearts, free from concepts and words, perceive the beauty of these bondless connections.
- The art of healing through dreaming, rituals, music, nature, and poetry helps us to experience the spaces outside of our minds.
- In these moments we are embraced and touched by the world, present and connected to an intelligent regenerative reality.
- Re-member to live the joy and aliveness of spirit, of a child, consciously manifesting without thought.

Chapter 6

Joyous Reconnections and Spontaneous Remissions

"I trapped my breath in the bellows of my throat:
a lamp blazed up inside, showed me who I really was.
I crossed the darkness holding fast to that lamp,
scattering its light-seeds around me as I went."[60]

– Lalla

I lay on the floor of the church hall in central London with 50 others, attending a weekend workshop on shamanism. It must have been about 2002. As I lay down and the large room went quiet, a voice inside me whispered, "Welcome home." I sat up with a start. Where did the voice come from? Did everyone hear it? It can't have been just me. The other attendees were still lying peacefully on their backs with their eyes closed, so I disregarded the welcome. It must have been my imagination.

It was one of the first conscious memories I have of hearing my inner voice guiding me along a path. I liked the idea that shamanism was the first spiritual path practiced over 100,000 years ago and that shamans were able to heal physical problems. How could I integrate this with my skills as a physiotherapist?

After the workshop, I looked more deeply into the meaning of a shaman. A shaman is someone who from experiential learning has the ability to effect change in their life force energy system and

[60] Naked Song: Lalla, Trans. Coleman Bark (Athens, GA: Maypop Books 1992)

who responds dynamically and optimally to the events that unfold around them. They work with the creative forces of nature and use this knowledge to assist others to heal the body. We all have this collective ability to direct the pervading life force. The Hawaiians call this energy 'mana.'

Still curious, I sought out YouTube videos and further reading about shamans. I had always loved stories from the Native American culture and the Australian Aboriginals. I had chosen to become a physiotherapist so I could work and visit the red earth of Australia. As I continued to read, I became ever more curious about the understanding that the indigenous peoples have of the world around us. The animist and shamans hold the view that every living thing has a spirit, and each has equal merit and so is held in mutual respect and love. Tim Ingold says of this animist view of life: "It is a way of being that is alive and open to a wonder of continuous birth. Life in short is a movement of opening, not of closure."[61] I was hooked.

Once I had encountered this mystical experience in the workshop, I wanted to experience more, as it seemed easy for me to connect to stones and to journey with a drumbeat. I took a few more day courses on connecting with the invisible realms. I stopped seeking the exact causes to why things happen; instead, I began to see that everything was an experience in waiting. I found that wanting to know exactly what will happen, to be certain of the future, to define it with expectations, whether it is for the next hour or next day or next week, limits these experiences and opportunities. This ability to open to any experience without limitations frees us from our own fears and self-doubt. It is an ability I am cultivating as it allows me to trust and feel safer even in unknown territory.

When I decided to write this book, the universe had already given me a team of personal spiritual guides to help. Encouragement and support arrived from many different sources, which spurred me on. I no longer wanted to negotiate with myself about any concerns I had in writing the book. Was it the right time? Did I

---

[61] Tim Ingold, *Being Alive: Essays on movement, knowledge and description* (Oxford: Routledge 2011).

have too many other responsibilities? Were the current medical dogmas putting me off? However, I decided to empower myself rather than wait for the acceptance of others. By listening to that intimate, but ever so loud inner voice, the mystical, spiritual part of myself grew stronger. I surrendered to this sense of knowing and put desire into action, facing all my inner obstacles and challenges as they arose, as I opened deeper to the research of helping myself and others.

As I became more present, I became more familiar with both the inner space of my body and the space around my body. By this, I mean the apparent space under my skin rather than the specifics of the organs. I learnt not only to experience the details of the sights and the sounds but also more of the external world, realizing that the silence that is present in the moments of complete stillness are opportunities of creative awareness and pivotal shifts.

It is in the joy of that silence that everything is to be found. It was hard at first to find and then remain in this place of stillness as our senses are drawn to certain distracting thoughts and images. Whenever I began to feel off-center and unclear, I would invite back the state of gentle focusing, receiving, listening, and transmitting. At first, I only remembered to do it when I was feeling grouchy, anxious, bored, or frustrated. I so wanted to feel more like my normal self again. As time progressed it became a natural place for me to drop into and regenerate.

As I continued my journeying in these silent spaces, there appeared a pause, a gap, as before birth and before death. The feeling of this gap was a homecoming of certainty that was such a comfort. This pregnant pause expanded and held me briefly in a new awareness before the energies dissolved. Creation is an orgasmic experience whether it is creating another human being, birthing a child or an idea, or recreating yourself. When you fully give to yourself this moment of change it happens time and time again. Spontaneous physical healing also occurs in these moments. It is to recognize something that is innately present, yet also intangible and difficult to grasp with words and emotions. For some this moment occurs when in a coma, before death or when suffering from an 'incurable disease' and then experiencing a remission. These times of letting go allow for new perceptions and for regeneration, healing and a new lease of life. None of us need to wait until our last few breaths to join in fully now. Spontaneous remissions are acts of acceptance of our DNA, our Divine Natural Arrangement.

We have the ability to plug ourselves into the infinite healing touch of the universe and experience the creative womb at any time. We can learn to trust and to feel more of this informational streaming within our bodies. I liken it to those science fiction films where the alien, or cybernetic half-human, returns to the workshop to plug into the system and get recharged. Glowing all over, it walks out freshly energized. Mind you, there is only so much information we can take in at any one time or we might blow a gasket! We can be depleted easily by this cosmic internet and become overloaded by the intensity of the human experience when we forget to stay centered in our true nature. These fluctuations in our energy state happen every minute of the day, many so subtle we do not notice them. Others are so dramatic and awesome we remember them forever. Gradually we learn to balance our worldly responsibilties with our need for inner reflection and quiet. Topping ourselves up regularly from the vast network of flowing energy around us continues to help me live with vitality and joy. The subtle essence of the natural world is one of my best therapists and is for many of my clients too.

CASE STUDY
Young Andrew makes friends with his hip

Andrew's mother, Jane, was worried about the bullying her son was experiencing in his class at school. She believed the right hip pain and disturbed sleep that Andrew had experienced for over a year was connected to it. She brought him to the clinic to see if I could help.

"So, Andrew, what does your hip want to make it feel better?" I asked, as I held it and moved it. It was a little sore moving in one particular direction.

"To climb a tree in my garden," he quickly replied.

I said, "Go on," encouraging him to imagine. He did this and sat on a branch and told me of the height he had reached and what he could see. I could tell he felt proud of his climbing and the good view he had achieved. He smiled at me.

"Does your hip want anything else to feel really happy?"

"I want to fly a kite from the tree," he said. "One with a pirate on it." He described it and watched it for a while blow in the wind. I continued to move his hip into and out of the area that was mildly sore.

"Anything else," I enquired?

"The sun to make it all warm and bright." He lay relaxing with these thoughts, watching and feeling the scene he had created.

Suddenly he said, "I let go of the kite and it has blown far away, I can't see it anymore." He came down from his tree, smiling, the sun still shining.

Jane called me three weeks later to say that Andrew's sleeping was much better with minimal disturbance and that he now rarely complained of the hip pain.

Bhutanese Adventures

I fell into a truly mystical experience when in Bhutan. I had visited this very magical kingdom in 2013 on a ten-day holiday and it presented me with many heart-opening experiences. I vowed to return as soon as possible. Within six months of returning home, an opportunity arose for me. On the spur of the moment, I took that opportunity and volunteered to give a talk on 'Health and energy; the body as an antenna,' at the First International Conference for Bhutanese Buddhist nuns. One of the aims of the conference was to inspire the younger nuns to share more of their gifts, both with their community and further afield on the world stage.

Eighty nuns from all over the world attended the conference. Some had travelled five days from the remote highlands of eastern Bhutan. I was only one of a handful of women at the conference who were not ordained. Surrounded by the collective energy of these beautiful women, I felt free and able to be myself. I did not realise why at the time, but on reflection I believe it was because I felt safe and happy being the woman and creator that I am.

There are only a handful of Buddhist nuns worldwide who have been recognized and honored by Buddhist authorities. The Venerable Jetsunma Tenzin Palmo is one of them. She is the subject of the book Cave in the Snow[62] and was the guest speaker at the conference. Jetsunma is English and grew up in the east end of London. In the 1960s, she knew she wanted to be a Buddhist nun, so she traveled to India where she entered a monastery. In response to the difficulties she faced as a woman in a male dominated society and wanting more seclusion, she spent 12 years on her own in a cave up a high mountain, learning the nature of her mind. She came to establish two nunneries, one in the Himalayas of India and one in Tibet. Financial support and teaching of monks in India and Tibet is common, whereas it is more difficult for nuns to find. Jetsunma is an inspiring heroine to me.

---

[62] Vicki Mackenzie, *Cave in the snow: a Western woman's quest for enlightenment* (London: Bloomsbury, 1999).

My presentation had been rescheduled for the third day, a fortuitous opportunity as the King's mother was present. She heard my talk and had witnessed the dialogue and resistant stance of the interpreter who happened to be the only psychiatrist in Bhutan. He chose to interpret some of my talk from his own viewpoint. That evening at the gala dinner, the King's mother invited me to her table. Naturally this is not what I encounter every day, so I was somewhat apprehensive when called over.

At the head table was Jetsunma, a woman with a powerful yet gentle presence who had been the keynote speaker of the three-day conference. I had spoken with her previously. She detected my nervousness as I stood by the table and simply smiled at me. I shall never forget those beams of golden light and the immense energy that emanated from her eyes. Suddenly I felt at ease and sat down next to the King's mother and began talking to her as if I were chatting to a friend in a coffee shop. She expressed an interest in the information in my talk and told me that the nuns had mastered this healing work years ago, as well as other skills such as the art of combustion and flying. I responded that I had better be careful! She was interested in my teaching in Bhutan. This gave me great confidence. She asked me to help a friend of hers who was experiencing pain that evening. Naturally I said yes, so together we went to the floor above and sat on the comfortable sofas and began the treatment session. As soon as we came down the royal party left the dinner banquet.

Looking back at my fear before speaking with the King's mother and my sudden relaxation after receiving Jetsunma's calming gaze, I was amazed by the sudden change in my energy and physiology. The anxiety associated with my racing thoughts and my increased breathing and heart rate all diminished in a flash of light, quite literally. What had happened? Had the light already existed and somehow I was suddenly sensitive to it as I became more present and calm? I shifted in response to my exchange with Jetsunma, changing from my state of fear to one of comfort, happily engaging in communication. The receiving of such a beautiful light fills me with gratitude and will stay with me for eternity.

On the last morning of the conference, I waved goodbye to the nuns. They were travelling to the capital Timphu for the National Day celebrations. I had decided to stay and walk in the local villages and follow the river upstream with the magnificent Himalayas as a backdrop. I was excited to explore more of the countryside on foot. Before leaving, Jetsunma came over and asked me why I had come? I was at a loss for words and am still discovering the unfolding answer.

Adventures on the Big Island of Hawai'i

In 2016, I was guided to visit the island chain of Hawai'i. I travelled those many miles to attend a retreat on the Big Island. In the end, I didn't take part. Instead, I listened and allowed the Divine Natural Arrangement to guide me. Through this I met many wonderful people, including Suzette, who introduced me to the magic of Hawai'i, and to Jack and Zae[63] who helped me to see the next path to take. What blessings and gratitude I give for the ability to listen to my inner guidance. The islands of Hawai'i, its ancestors, and peoples have helped me so much.

On arrival, the nature of these islands speaks so loudly one can only listen. It's simply unavoidable. The Big Island of Hawai'i has ten of the 14 climates of the world, five volcanoes, and the clearest view of the solar system I have ever seen. There are dolphins, whales, and turtles to wonder at. The fertility and energy of the land is both fierce and awesome, continually producing with abundance.

In Hawai'i, as in Great Britain, weather changes are a constant source of talk and amazement. We become used to the four seasons in one day and sometimes in the same hour. The ancient Gods, the Akua of the Hawaiian Islands, represent the forces of nature as well as other symbolic meanings. Hawaiians have more than 200 different words for rain, showing the importance this life-giving water holds for them. They have studied nature so skillfully that they have identified and named more than 600

---

63 Muaisa Hale Pule https://www.muaisa.org/

different types of wind. Predicting the weather accurately is nigh impossible and knowing that helps us adjust to its unexpected fluctuations on a regular basis. If only our minds experienced such changes as gracefully as we do the weather. To be able to experience and accept equally the grey, cloudy skies, as well as those rarer clear blue sky never-ending English days is a true gift. Buddhist teachings remind us that our minds are like the weather: thoughts and emotions come and go, they are impermanent and as such it is wise not to fixate on any—all storms do pass.

Rainbows in Hawai'i are very common and are looked upon as blessings from above. Sun and water fall from the sky to earth creating light of all colors in every direction. Double rainbows appear regularly. Did you know that if we look at a rainbow, we all see it differently due to our position in relation to the sun, yet perhaps deep within we acknowledge it in the same way? Viewing ourselves as rainbows, we are the beginning and ending and anywhere we choose to be in-between. They appear from no point in particular and then disappear from view beyond the horizon. Even though we do not directly see the full circle of a rainbow we can experience the completion of that whole sphere. We accept with ease the beauty and simplicity of this natural phenomenon of water and fire and like the rainbow, we can also learn to do this within ourselves. Every encounter in life is a blessing, everything is conceived to help us and to see the reality at the core of our being and inviting us to thrive both individually and together.

When I arrived, the land of Hawai'i seemed very familiar to me with the fragrant exotic smells of the plumeria and pikake flowers. It fascinated me. Great swathes of land are covered by black lava flows that emerged from the center of the earth. Pele, the fire goddess of the volcano, is still very active on the Big Island of Hawai'i in the continually erupting Kilauea volcano. She helps illuminate, cover, and burn all that is no longer needed, creating the land anew many times over. This experience of raw and primeval creation is very much the energy that I found. The lave flows have minds and energies of their own. One type is called a'a as it is jagged and hurts to walk on it. The other is gently undulating with swirls like you would see in the icing on top of a cake. It is called pahoehoe.

I loved the nature of the Big Island in all its resonant forms. The beauty of the trees, the ocean, and the skies. The Hawaiian culture has a great reverence for all of nature as it is to them a true reflection of God. To live in harmony with the abundance of all that is around you brings you closer to the God within. The Hawaiians talk about a vertical time, perfect balance connecting the flowing data that is ever present and available to us. This flow holds no memories of past or future.

The Essence of the Hawaiian Spirit

Residents of Hawai'i greet each other with the word 'aloha,' a word that has many meanings. It is a recognition of the breath of God in all living things and it is also a welcome greeting to share this presence. Aloha is a code for life: unselfish, truthful, patient, respectful and accepting. It is humbling yet strong and tender, nurturing, and enduring. 'Hā' is the breath of life, and it is also the number four. It is a way of life representing the gratitude of connection to ourselves, nature, and others.

The earth is highly valued by the Hawaiians, and she is always consulted before building on any land. All land is sacred and is for us to protect and use wisely. We are its caretakers, it is a gift, our home, just like the personal home of our bodies. We are simply looking after it for future generations. We do not own it. When the land is not honored and included in decision making, problems arise, such as failed business, time delays, and sickness for those working on the land. In the same way we are unique beings, so is the earth with its own requests. Some land has innate healing properties, some are naturally magnificent in their wildness, whilst others love to be tended to and shared and cherished for all of the community. Sites for the Heiau, the sacred temples of worship of the Hawaiian Gods, are chosen for their spiritual energy and may be on a clearing of a hillside or by a beach. Heiau are present on all the Hawaiian Islands.

The energy arising from the earth in Hawai'i is intense. A friend said to me, it is as if the earth is pushing the houses off the land. At first, I became very anxious and fearful surrounded by this intense energy. It was familiar, yet unknown at the same time and I began to realize I was awakening to a more profound inner journey. One morning as I sat on the grass after my yoga routine, ready to meditate, I felt these surges of energetic life flow through my body. I held onto the green tufts and breathed out to release the overwhelm. It felt as if I was about to take off! That life force, the pulse of the earth, so palpable, alive, and invigorating awakened my body. It spoke volumes to me but at that time, I could not decipher it. As I began to relax, I grew accustomed to feeling the changing pulse of the earth and became even more curious of my relationship to this land.

After a year of getting to know the land, she spoke to me in a different way. It was a beautiful afternoon, perfect for a relaxing swim in the bay after hot work in the garden. I was swimming, returning to the inlet where I had started. As I looked up to make sure I was still heading in the right direction, I heard a voice inside say, "Danger, be careful." I glanced around: no sharks, no high winds, the swell of the waves was no different. What could it mean? I continued to swim in a leisurely way back to the shore. I commented to the caretaker of the park that it was a perfect still afternoon. I walked back home to take a shower. While I was immersed under the water, the ground started to shake, and we experienced a 5.3 magnitude earthquake. There followed a loud crashing as rocks on the hillside from six locations slid down into the bay. Though my swim did not take me where the rockslides happened, I had been supported and informed of the potential danger that was to follow. What was it that had spoken to me? What was I resonating with? Nature had spoken through me.

My friend Suzette took me to many sacred sites on the Big Island of Hawai'i where I experienced events that had happened in the past and received powerful messages. The land and rocks hold the energy, memories, and knowledge of times gone by, just like our own bodies.

The Power of the Ocean

Surfing is one of the many ocean activities that are part of being Hawaiian. Young children learn to respect the waves that brought them to these shores and still supply them with fun and an abundance of marine life. To really know the waves is to swim in and to be with them, feeling, studying, and watching their form, riding them, and experiencing the exhilaration of togetherness as you choose that perfect wave. Sitting and waiting for the next cycle of waves to manifest requires patience, awareness, and perfect timing. It is a practice for the waves we ride in life.

I found myself learning this art of togetherness on a paddleboard. I had sailed a dinghy and windsurfed in the UK and loved the feeling of the salty sun-kissed wind and water on my body and in my hair. This relationship of the paddleboard with the water was different from that of my other crafts. I was now without the assistance of the wind in a sail, and I steadily learnt to make the new connections. With a paddleboard, balancing on the surface of the water was critical to harnessing the connection with the elements and the deeper undercurrents that at first seemed invisible.

To the north of Kealakekua Bay rises the Pali, a sacred elevation where the bones of some of the Hawaiian chiefs are buried. Below, at sea level, is a small piece of British soil upon which a monument has been erected to Captain Cook. He met his demise here in 1779. The presence of the Pali is constantly changing, and I make it a point to watch whenever I can. At dusk, the fading sunlight plays the artist, experimenting with the colored fabric on the hillside. Glorious.

The paddleboard and I were skimming gently across the waves and water enjoying the simplicity of our friendship. I began to admire and feel the magnificence of the Pali and the strength that it held as we approached it. Suddenly, as I placed my paddle in the water, I was catapulted forward a good four feet and landed in the sea under the cliffs. It was as if the rocks had been listening to me and wanted to show me that they did indeed hold great power. I started laughing and I heard the echo reflect from the hillside back to me.

In Kealekekua Bay, pods of dolphins come into rest after a night of fishing. The bay is a beautiful marine sanctuary. The Hawaiian name means "Pathway to the Gods." One full moon morning on Thanksgiving Day I purposefully arose early as I knew the dolphins would come in that morning. I saw the sunrise behind me, and a pink glow filled the skies. The air was still. I sat on the large pebbles and closed my eyes and gave thanks for being in such a wonderful, special place. Some time later I opened them again and the dolphins were visible in the bay in front of me. I quickly put on my fins and mask and swam out. They were close to the shore this morning.

I waited and soon one spinner dolphin came up to me. She put her nose right in front of mine inviting me to engage with her. I was so shocked. She moved back a little, turned and gave a wiggle, so I did too. I put my head deeper into the water, she swam back, and we locked eyes, magnetized. It felt so special. I noticed the markings on her back as if she had been pierced by a spear on the right side. I observed the way she nodded her beak up and down and felt the response in my body. She swam away. The same dolphin came up to me again 20 minutes later, followed by about 30 others emerging from the sand bed below, swimming in a vortex around me. Dolphins were everywhere. I twisted and turned in an attempt to see them all, wanting to spin with them. When I clambered back up onto the rocks an hour later, I was trembling with so much joy and lightness it lasted for many hours. Since then, I can still feel the dolphins swimming through my body.

I was becoming acutely aware that my body was beginning to pick up more information from the environment. Sometimes I would resonate with it and at other times not! The body can detect anything we ask it to if we care to pay attention. Our minds interpret, and we negotiate the response. Our hearts are aware and wait for us to listen. To elicit the union of our Triune self—body, mind, and heart (see Chapter 4)—we must become silent, still, and open, and be present with the flow, pulse, and rhythm of energy inside and out. In this space, I feel safe, for the earth holds the essence of the greatest Mother and protector there is, always present in all ways. This comfort of the abundance of the earth fills my belly.

Ancient Stories of Hawai'i

On these islands, myths and legends like the story of the bowl of light are still used to convey wisdom. Knowledge is handed down by sharing stories, dancing hula, and in chants. The Hawaiians are also said to have hidden knowledge out in the open for all to see. What did all this mean? I was intrigued. When I was younger, I would dream and visit a magical place. It reminded me of the Shangri-La I had seen in the movies, that place of peace and beauty where everything was divinely possible. When I started to read about Hawaiian legends, I learned that the people refer to a "land of the invisible creative spirit" called Kanehunamoku.

Ohana: The Hawaiian Family

There is a Hawaiian proverb that says, "You are a chief because of your people." The Hawaiians live as a 'community of family' with interdependence, mutual respect, kindness, loyalty and affection. This not only includes blood family and neighbors, but also nature and the surrounding lands, the stars and the cosmos, and the spirit world of the ancestors. The Hawaiian people live closely with nature and the spirits that reside in everything that surrounds them. Personal and family prayers and chants, pule and songs, 'mele', so named in Hawaii, remind each of us to reach for help outside of ourselves. In doing so, we honor, maintain, and strengthen these connections to community. When we live in harmony with all, ensuring open and loving connections, we, and all of the human races thrive.

We all came from the same root.
Let us remember and live as such.

A Hawaiian healer is called a 'kahuna' and the translation means the keeper of wisdom and hidden secrets; revealing the light where it is dim. There are kāhuna, experts in other professions as well. The kahuna is invited into the community to help settle disputes in families and between families and connects with the forces of the Divine, the land, and nature. If an individual family member remains ill after receiving Lomilomi massage and after taking medicinal herbs, then pule and Ho'oponopono are used with the extended family. Hawaiians believe that the physical body will only heal fully if the mental, emotional, and spiritual parts of the person are united first.

The Hawaiian healing practise of Ho'oponopono, 'making things right,' is a beautiful process of mending broken connections. When felt deeply in the heart and breathed by the body, it is a profound renewal of energy for the bowl of light. There are many aspects to the prayer as it unfolds. A contemporary form of the prayer can include four powerful phrases of healing:
"I love you."
"I am sorry."
"Please forgive me."
"Thank you.'

With Ho'oponopono you make things right, not only with yourself, but with your family and friends, the land, and the wider community by acknowledging past traumas held in the land and bones of our bodies. It is a release and healing of transgenerational traumas. Living your life pono, or in a right or moral way, ensures continued connection with the Divine values in you. To do this, we must take responsibility and forgive ourselves when necessary, letting go of inner conflict and asking the Divine in us and in others to forgive us, so that we can release any grievances and disputes that cause illness. Once the emotional charge is released, the remaining void is filled with a healing light. The Hawaiians believe, as do other indigenous peoples, that these prayers, spoken with reverence, extend healing to the whole ancestral family, including many generations deceased as well as those yet to come. This is epigenetic healing.

Try this inner dialogue when called to use the prayer:

> I love you, that part of me that feels sad, angry, doubting, confused....
>
> I am sorry for not having seen you earlier, for ignoring you, for the dispute and separation I/we feel and or I/we may have caused.
>
> Thank you for showing to me that part of me that needs healing and listening to.
>
> Thank you for the healing connections I am receiving now.
>
> Please forgive me and everyone else involved with the problem.
>
> You may also want to ask, taking full responsibility for the situation you are in, "How may I help? What do you need? What can I do?"

I use this prayer of Ho'oponopono and the dialogue to help myself at times of self-doubt and to hold myself with compassion.[64] It is also useful when I recognize a situation that requires a new perspective, perhaps where I have been resentful or fearful and not speaking from a centered place of truth and connection. This process helps us take responsibility for all our encounters in the world and provides us and others with a means of continual healing. It is one way to change the collective consciousness that we are all a part of.

Ho'oponopono was useful to me with a recurring dilemma of not feeling good enough. I was sitting in Hawaiian paradise surrounded by the birds singing and the tropical elements voicing their contentment and yet part of my inner voice was repeatedly doubting myself. Could I really write this book? Could it be of use to others to help them heal themselves? I was in that anxious place, confused and temporarily floundering, without the steady

---

[64] This is my interpretation and may not reflect the original intention of the prayer

balance of my internal GPS. I thought to myself, I must stop listening to the voices saying I am missing information, not the right person to write, not good enough, not ready, not at the right time... an endless preoccupation with the negatives and reasons for inaction. Using Concentra and Ho'oponopono, I centered once again in my co-creative flow.

I listened to the heaviness in my body, my separated heart, the anxiousness in my belly, the doubts, the disconnection with nature, the joy and beauty no longer there. I gave thanks, said sorry to that part I had ignored and was now calling for my help, cradling and loving the separated parts. We sat together for a while. I explored outside of myself and found the direction of the space that was in relationship with my feeling sense and invited it to me, giving thanks for the source of reconnection. I waited. I knew that space well. It had helped me come through many fearful and overwhelming periods of my life. I felt new areas of my body responding, my awareness exploring new places. I felt the inner and outer spaces drawing together, gradually uniting and dissolving.

A wave of heat flooded my face and upper body, my ears buzzed at a higher pitch. I felt energy move in a figure of eight move between my ears and a gust of wind blew through the palm leaves telling me a change had occurred. I felt the coldness of space inside my body and noticed myself holding my breath and so I breathed again. My jaw was tight. I watched my breath, and the image of the dolphins that I had experienced previously came to me. A massive pod was swimming beneath me, resting after a night of fishing. Dolphins in this dream-like state are still aware of others around them. I continued to experience the space inside, listening intently to the sound in my body. I could have believed I had tinnitus hearing the ringing in my ears. I became conscious of my own quiet awareness as I became the dolphin moving through the water with my family. The velvety water enlivened and delighted my body. As the moon disappeared behind the Pali, the sun came out and shone through the water, the sand beneath became alive and a curtain of rising bubbles appeared in front of me of various sizes and shone with golden, blue and pink light. My preoccupation with doubts had vanished.

Navigating Uncharted Waters

The Polynesians do navigation very well. They are experts in it. How else could they find these islands in the middle of the Pacific? Some say that these eight Hawaiian islands are in the middle of nowhere, but they are connected to everything, the vastness of the waters that are both at the center of and surround the 'Ring of Fire'. This is a horseshoe shaped area in the Pacific Ocean where the majority of the earth's volcanic activity and earthquakes occur in response to the movement of many tectonic plates. It is a place of continual creativity.

Hawaiians have revived their traditional navigational skills with the Hōkūle'a voyaging canoe, which has already travelled to many countries teaching young people the art of knowing where they are without the use of a compass. Knowledge and study of the cycles of the tides, the different types of winds, and positions of the stars allows for accurate location of place and time, referencing where you have come from, and where you are heading. They trust in their ability to be guided to safety. This trust has allowed the Hawaiians to explore uncharted waters connecting to previously hidden lands. We can take many lessons from the skills of these travelers and use them to discover previously uncharted territory within ourselves. Some say that we are that canoe in which we journey into the cosmos exploring the stars. I write about our internal GPS and navigational compass more fully in the next chapter.

CASE STUDY
James talks to his upper back to find his direction

A physiotherapy colleague had a six-month history of pain in the right side of his mid back. He had been unable to run and had to take time off work. Despite previous treatment he still felt pain on breathing and leaning backwards and following a day of working with patients. He could not feel his core abdominal stomach muscles working strongly despite going to the gym, exercising and focusing on them. This worried him.

I asked him to go onto his hands and knees, feeling into the discomfort, in his middle back. I prodded it a little to make sure he really felt it. James connected to it directly and then up to his head and down to the bottom of his spine. He experienced the new tingling sensation move through his body. I invited him to direct the new sensation and breathe it into the other areas of his body that had not yet received the different energy. He wiggled, relaxed, breathed gently in and out and experienced. Finally, James centered himself in all directions of the compass.

After a couple of minutes, he stood up and though he tried many times, twisting and turning could not feel the pain again. What delighted James even more was the fact that his core was working spontaneously and felt strong.

The next day he demonstrated the improvement in his movement, but still had some ache after the long day's work. He noticed it especially when reaching forward at a particular angle. James had some reluctance moving into that direction and space. I did not ask him specifically what this direction and angle represented as he expressed the desire to be able to go there without pain.

Working with Concentra, James reached for the aching space in front of him, which he also described as a block of wood. He focused inside his body feeling both the ache in his mid-spine and the other constricted areas in the backs of his upper legs, particularly on the right. He alternated experiencing the inside and outside energy, breathing gently all the time. He moved further into the space in front of him, feeling his core supporting him in the direction he desired. The two energies seamlessly working together created the experience James wanted.

Two days later, James had little memory of the pain. He realised that his breathing was restricted and so was paying attention to improve this cycle when it became less rhythmical and felt pressured. James moved through this 'stuckness' and is now happily working in New Zealand.

"Love is of all the passions the strongest,
for it attacks simultaneously
the head, the heart, and the senses."

– Lao Tzu

Thoughts to Germinate

- The beauty, aliveness, and continual flux of the natural world helps us to reconnect with the spiritual aspect of ourselves.
- Honoring and working with nature and its creations restores our body's health.
- Recognizing your internal GPS helps you to ride the challenging waves and undercurrents of life.
- You can shine your inner light more brightly every time you empty your bowl of light.
- With the unfolding of your Divine Natural Arrangement spontaneous healing occurs.
- The power of prayer, chants and the Hawaiian pule of Ho'oponopono reconnects you to the power of healing presence.

Chapter 7

Mirrors, the Moon, Stars, and Immunity

"Beauty is eternity gazing at itself in a mirror. But you are eternity and you are the mirror."[65]

– Kahlil Gibran

Mirrors help us to see ourselves and others. They appear in front of us every day as helpful tools of reflection. In my process of self-discovery, this metaphor has helped me become clearer and healthier in myself. Our bodies are mirrors and reflections of all we become aware of on earth, our relationships and in the space of the sky above. The stars, planets, and constellations exchange with us their powerful energies, too. The creative power and beauty of the universe is evident in our vitality and zest for living.

Mirror therapy can be an effective treatment for individuals with chronic pain. In amputees and paraplegics who continue to feel unremitting pain in their lost limbs, using a mirror to show them an image of their healthy limb can help to reduce their pain. For an amputee, seeing a full limb moving in a mirror in place of the missing limb can trick the brain into believing it is present and whole. This new awareness reduces the perception of pain. For paraplegics who feel pain in their legs but are unable to feel them connected to their bodies, watching a video of someone else walking whilst they are standing supported can reduce pain and bring with it a feeling of well-being. Seeing and remembering the

[65] Kahlil Gibran, *The Prophet* (Penguin, 1992).

normal patterns of sensation and movement associated with the limb helps to rebuild healthy connections in the body.

I have an amazing friend, Beka, who is a portrait painter. When studying her pieces, I ask myself, what is it I see in the picture before me? Perhaps it reflects that part of myself I recognize in the face of another and other faces I have not identified with. Her art captures so many facets that in her work we all catch a unique glimpse of humanity in the one face. In a well composed piece, the space around the sitter becomes an extension of her being. This is the same space that amputees and paraplegics engage with to relieve their limb pain. These questions and observations are so important to contemplate, for they guide us to see the true beauty of all that lies before our eyes.

Look at yourself in the mirror today.
Soften your eyes, catch a glimpse of what is
really true for you

Have you heard the expression, 'You are a real pill'? It has such a depth of truth. We are those pills to each other, mirrors, antidotes, and safe spaces for others to heal their ills, to connect with themselves again. Do we give thanks for these opportunities of loving and new connections? We might not like some of the mirrors that are held up and pills we are asked to take and discard their wisdom, preferring to stick with what we already know.

The Hawaiians tell us the tale of Pohaku Kilo, the Mirror Stone. I came across this when visiting the museum on the island of Lāna'i and this exhibit grabbed my attention. The story tells of a dense stone that is polished with kukui nut oil. This is a sacred oil from the kukui tree on the islands and is known for its ability to illuminate the light within. The polished stone is put into water and the tradition says that if you look not at the stone, but at the surface of the water, there you will find the reflection of yourself.

CASE STUDY
June's body experiences the loss of her dog

"I don't know what is wrong, all my joints are seizing up, painful and swollen and I just want to lie in bed."

June told me that she had just lost Sammy, her dog, a Jack Russell who had been her constant companion for 13 years. Since she had retired, she had devoted her time to looking after him and keeping fit by walking regularly. He had been her confidant and part of her identity. Now she was unable to go upstairs without pain, spending much of her time sitting or lying in bed. Within a matter of weeks, June's physical state had taken a dramatic turn. She was now under a rheumatologist being investigated for an autoimmune systemic inflammatory condition. I did not treat June for she preferred to continue with the plan of action her specialist had provided.

June was devastated by the death of her dog and could not envisage a life without him. She was equally fearful about the health challenges she was now facing. Her home inside and out were unfamiliar places, unrecognizable, an unexpected turn of events for which she had no coping strategy.

Witnessing this many years ago helped me appreciate the fragility of the human psyche and the rapidity of the body's response to trauma. There are many challenges and transitions to navigate as we move through the necessary changes of the cycle of death, rebirth, and regeneration.

Our Bodies' Connections to the Heavens

Hawaiian Honoring of the Moon

The moon is like a mirror: we are only able to see the surface because it reflects light from the sun back to earth. It is impossible to capture its essence in a bottle or jar for that radiant light far outshines any boundary you care to give it.

Hina is the Hawaiian Goddess of the Moon. She is one of the oldest female energies in Hawaiian culture, important for healing and bringing to us all great knowledge and awareness. Through the energy of the word 'Hina' we nurture our sacred space; we can stand calmly with inner strength for all that we believe in. The myth says that Hina arose from the depths of the ocean and rode on a rainbow to reach the moon, escaping from her earth husband. She is the radiant beauty in all of us, carrying many forms and colors. Some sources say Hina presides over the earth and water elements, bringing health and wealth to all.

The Hawaiians believe that the start of each new day begins after the sun has set. They work with the phases of the moon to guide them daily through their lives. The moon cycle is used to determine the best times to fish, plant, or harvest certain food crops, as well as when medicinal herbs are best cut for maximum benefit. Each of the 30 days in the moon calendar has a specific name reflecting the deep significance of this cycle for the Hawaiians. The 29th day of the moon cycle is called Mauli. The term relates to the fontanel on a baby's head, as well as the name given to the integration of the three energy centres of the body which I discussed in Chapter 3.

Moon Reflections

Through our bodies we feel the influence of the magnetic push and pull of the moon, so honoring and living in harmony with this naturally occurring cycle will bring us great benefit. As we embody both the dark and the light phases of the moon and the halo of the moon during an eclipse, we become one with the inside and the outside of our bodies and begin to understand the magnetic cycles of time and space. There are seven days to each of the four phases of the moon. Working with the energy of the moon is one way that helps with self-inquiry, daily contemplations, and improving our physical health. Journaling as we develop a relationship with the different phases of the moon is a useful pastime.

- What phase is the moon in now? What do I want to create or what do I want to diminish in this quarter?
- How do I feel and know myself with this light reflection?
- Which phase of the moon do I reflect today?
- What part of me do I want to reveal to another?
- How much am I willing to reveal and expose to help myself and others to shine?
- Am I balanced, more light or dark, crescent to the left, or right?
- What is behind me guiding my reflection?

If we cover our lightness with darkness, we do not shine, yet we are containers of both the light and dark.

Cosmic Mirrors and Mirror Particles

We've seen how the moon is a mirror on the earth so let's expand the idea of further guidance from the skies.

The solar plexus is located within our abdominal and heart regions where we measure and then filter and digest the world around us. It is where we choose what we desire to ingest and assimilate to help us thrive as a contributory, connected being in the world. When we look at the cosmic solar system—the sun, moon, planets and constellations, and the galaxy beyond—we witness in ourselves the sum of all cosmic motion. Start to communicate with the stars above you, for they have much wisdom to share. Space scientists can observe motion of star systems with arrays of many telescopes and mirrors measuring and recording the interactive pattern of light waves from the stars in a process called 'astronomical interferometry.' Our bodies also receive and integrate light information from different reference points; it is our unique blueprint of this planetary map of light.

It has been suggested that subatomic particles in the universe have mirror partners. Mirror particles have right hand interactions whilst ordinary particles have left-handed ones. If the symmetry between the two particles is broken, they lose contact. When the separated particles become aware of each other, the distance is resolved and balance is restored. This is a way for us to harmonize our bodies when we feel off center. We reach for the 'complimentary particle' by using Concentra and return ourselves to the space of connected wholeness.

Try this exercise to familiarize yourself with how to connect to mirror particles:

> Sit quietly and breathe with your feet on the floor connecting to the pulse of the earth and the sky above. Watch your breath. Notice the length of the inhale and exhale and the pause between the two. Continue for four minutes noticing how you feel, as your whole body breathes with this changing space connecting you to yourself and the universe. (Alternatively use Exercise A on page 165 to drop into a state of relaxed awareness).
>
> Choose a situation or a health challenge for which you desire a shift. From this place of stillness, and initially with your eyes closed, look around with your inner eyes to discover the location of the blocked energy and then locate the solution to resolving this blockage, either from inside or outside your body, or both. Breathe into these places to heighten your

connection and bring more energy and informational structure to the new awareness.

Does the breath of information want to move up or down the body? In or out? Left, or right? Back to front? Is it changing direction? Breathe with it following the movement for as long as possible.

The Quantum World and Its Link to Concentra

Our physical bodies are like quantum computers, and as such they can examine all the possible futures they expose themselves to. The more we bring acceptance or flow into our being, the easier it becomes to choose wisely and become a cooperative quorum of directed action to benefit the whole.

Black Holes – The Space Between Stars

Ancient civilizations believed that black holes were portals to new dimensions. Black holes contain light but hold so much gravitational pull that the light is unable to escape. They eat dead stars and debris, growing bigger, and they expand without actually increasing in volume. Black holes display a toroid field, the same movement that is produced by the heart and mitochondria. Stars move around black holes in the spherical cloud in a rosette pattern, similar to the flower of life. It is said that dark matter holds the fifth energetic elemental force in the universe, also known as ether, plasma, and potentiality. The balanced combination of the four elements is space-creating Quintessence, the perfect spirit concealed in all things.

I love this analogy that the light is present even in the dark. I like to remember this, especially on challenging days when I feel that my glass is half empty. Expansion and contraction in space is seen in the death and birth of new stars and on earth and white or black diamonds. Similarly, our cells grow and die and are replaced, after which our vibrating DNA antennae attune to the new halo of frequencies around them. We enter a new wormhole. In that instant our perceptions, beliefs, emotions, and physical bodies recalibrate.

"Nothing can dim the light that shines from within."

– Maya Angelou

On April 10, 2019, the first ever recorded image of a black hole was released to the public. The image was created from recordings taken by an array of eight terrestrial telescopes, collectively known as the Event Horizon Telescope, two of which are located on the sacred volcano of Mauna Kea on Hawai'i. This new black hole, located at the center of the M87 galaxy in the constellation Virgo, has been named Powehi. This word comes from an important ancient Hawaiian creation chant, the Kumulipo. Powehi means the "Embellished dark source of unending creation." This is a remarkable name and reminds us of the wisdom of our ancestors and of our own unending source of creative abilities found within the darkness.

I cherish that part of me that is this mystery. My creation is forever unfolding, and like a black hole, ever expanding, swallowing stars, adding more light energy as it funnels down and around into the darkness.

"When I see I am nothing, that is wisdom
When I see I am everything, that is love
Between those two, my life moves" [66]

– Nisargadatta Maharaj

[66] Sri Nisargadatta Maharaj, *I Am That* (Mumbai: Chetana Publishing, 1999).

Navigating With The Stars

"We need to start thinking beyond the physical body of who we are. I am a mother, grandmother. But there is not a moment in my life that I separate myself from a star being."

– Grandmother Flordemayo

Cygnus, the swan constellation, contains one of three stars that make up the 'Navigator Triangle,' which was a reference point for celestial navigators before the use of radar. Aboriginal tradition says that Cygnus is a connecting bridge to other dimensions, a signpost to the galactic equator. In ancient Hindu astrology it is known as the 'Brahma Muhurta' and represents the 'moment of the universe.' Solar winds and radio waves from here can be felt by us on earth. It has been a useful signpost for me in my use of Concentra and on my journey of discovery.

On the rose of the Ring Nebula of the wing of Cygnus sits a blue star Uli, the sacred name for an important Hawaiian goddess. She is said by some to be the highest emanating force of the Divine feminine and by her primordial nature takes on many forms.[67]

We are now living in a time for us all to remember, forgive, and bring back into the light all that we have been told to forget. Uli has returned to remind us how to birth ourselves as we travel the journey of life. Feel the essence of her hidden beauty travelling across the night skies.

"The stars are like letters that inscribe themselves at every moment in the sky. Everything in the world is full of signs. All events are coordinated. All things depend on each other. Everything breathes together" [68]

---

[67] Hank Wesselman, *The Bowl of Light: Ancestral Wisdom from a Hawaiian Shaman* (Louisville, CO: Sounds True, 2011): 178, 264.

[68] Plotinus, Stephen Mackenna, and John M. Dillon. *The Enneads.* (London, Penguin, 1991) II, 3, 7

Finding your internal compasses

"As above, so below, as within, so without, as the universe, so the soul..."

– Hermes Trismegistus

Like the indigenous tribes of today that connect with natural elements in nature to inform their understanding of spiritual forces, Concentra works in the same way, by connecting to natural elements to identify healing forces. During the renaissance period and earlier, the philosophers and scholars also connected and worked with the elements through the practice of spiritual alchemy.[69]

The Emerald Tablet of Hermes Trismegistus discusses the seven working principles of the universe and reading the text may illuminate questions for you to explore. The fifth Principle of Rhythm states: "Everything flows, out and in; the pendulum-swing manifests in everything; the measure of the swing to the right is the measure of the swing to the left—rhythm compensates."

To the alchemist, the principle of rhythm reflects movement between two polar opposites, such as sadness and joy. When we use this wisdom and awareness as a way of navigating the world we can learn and move through all situations. The swinging pendulum and the movement of the atoms take on a new pattern, our mental chatter quietens and our physicality changes. We return to our inherent rhythm.

The question of rhythm is perhaps something we do not readily remember, nor harmonize with and follow. Within us it is the

---

[69] Mary the prophetess, who lived between the first and third centuries, has been heralded as one of the first true alchemists. Her message: "The vessel of Hermes which the stoics (scientists) have concealed is the measure of your fire," is a true reflection of her understanding of the principles of alchemical change.

rhythms of the heart, breath, and body that govern the pattern of the EM field radiating from us and the frequencies we attract back to us.

This reminds me of a one-line comment a kumu hula (hula teacher) from the Hulihe'e Palace in Hawaii said to me when I asked him if I could learn the hula with him, "There must be a balance between the right and left sides." I am cultivating this modus operandi so that one day I may learn hula.

Flower of Life

The medicine wheel is used by many peoples all around the world as a compass to assist them in their deepening and honoring of connection to these forces and to their own spiritual essence. The compass points representing the four elements, the phases of the moon, sections of the day, and seasons, are all representations of the number four. Teachings on and around the medicine wheel are very important to us and help us to remember that we too have this innate ability of co-creating with the elements and forces of the cosmos the conditions for health in ourselves and others. My compass has guided me to experience the changing forces from each compass direction whilst living and listening to the land of Hawaii. It has taught me where I am not looking, my blind spots, and to identify my long-held unhelpful behaviors and beliefs. It has also taught me which directions and elements can help me.

As we practice the art of receiving and exchanging energetic information, we continually regenerate ourselves and re-establish our health. This is a continuous lifelong study of revelations, and it requires us to shift our behaviour and patterns of living to engage with life afresh at every moment. As we recalibrate our compasses and find that stillness in the storm, our internal home and health will beneficially change, as will the soil of Mother Earth. With the continual change of the earth's axis, our own spin shifts too. The Inuits confirm these changes, having observed that the sun rises and sets in a new place and that their prevailing wind is now blowing from another direction. Geologists also concur that the earth's magnetic field is changing. In fact, magnetic north has moved into the eastern hemisphere driven by a tug of war between streams of liquid iron under Canada and Siberia.[70] As I have shared, our bodies hold the substance magnetite, the same mineral that can be found in the rocks, soil, and in the air we all breathe. So, as the magnetic field of the earth changes, this will have an effect on our own internal compass. Becoming aware of the benefit of acknowledging these changes helps us to adapt to new challenges to our health and even to our society.

I choose to look at my own compass, aligning my direction wherever I am. I choose my own ley lines as I follow Mother Earth's pulsations and wobbles. I make friends with the Tropics of Cancer and Capricorn. I adjust to the stars and the new moons, the tides and winds that pull, so I can remain present and true, safe, and whole for as much of the time as possible.

The water pushes me, the wind blows me,
and the tides move me, and I am still.

---

[70] Alexandra Witze, "Earth's Magnetic Field Is Acting up and Geologists Don't Know Why", *Nature* 565, no. 7738 (January 1, 2019): 143–45.

Our Amazing Immune System

The immune system is our internal mirror of who and what we perceive ourselves to be in relation to the outside environment. It is a measure of how we respond to and integrate the differences that we encounter. Everything we experience affects our immune system. I am not only talking about bacteria, fungi, and viruses, but also our beliefs, mental images we construct, stories, and hidden, unhelpful behavioral traits. Just like viruses, this information within us lies hidden, dormant in our cells until we choose to look, and then an opening arises for us to know ourselves better and to grow in awareness. Some believe that viruses appear as evolutionary upgrades to systems.

Our immune system is intimately connected to both our mind and body. In the medical world this field of research is called psychoneuroimmunology (PNI). It was first thought that the immune system was present in small, isolated pockets of the body, but we know now it is everywhere. The innate immune system actively supports us in our early years releasing specialised protector cells. In part, it resides in our thymus gland under our breastbone. Our immune system also has an adaptive part which monitors and responds to all our worldly encounters and remembers past experiences. The innate and adaptive parts work together to keep us healthy and engaged with life.

Under certain conditions, the immune system can enter an overactive and self-destruct mode and can start to attack our own cells. In such cases, parts of our immune system believe we are, or have, a foreign invader. This failure to recognize parts of ourselves can create stress. If we are in a state of overwhelm or fear, our bodies will put more energy towards fighting the enemy and less energy on regenerating. Our immune cells may attack specific organs, joints, and tissues. Why do they do this and how do they choose which area to target? I have been fascinated by these autoimmune (AI) diseases, those 'syndromes' or groups of symptoms defined by a label. Included in this group are chronic fatigue syndrome, fibromyalgia, thyroiditis, Sjogren's syndrome, scleroderma, and rheumatoid arthritis, to name but a few. I have worked with them for years, preferring to help with the symptoms rather than the disease label. It is interesting to note that the majority of AI diseases are seen in women.[71]

As individuals, we develop fixed, limited views of ourselves, including our bodies, which bear no relationship to the wealth of our wonderous being. Our bodies show us where we are at odds with parts of ourselves. In fact, many of us do not even like our bodies. When we address these disparities, we see ourselves clearly and the body stops fighting itself; there is nothing to protect ourselves from, and new feelings, perceptions, and awareness become available.

It is thought by some that our stress response may be genetically determined, and as such we respond to events in the same way as our ancestors. Research shows that after a population has lived through a period of starvation or war, the physiological response of their descendants years later still reflects a relationship to the trauma. The offspring show an increased sensitivity to fear and lack of food, which is experienced in the physiology of their body and in their behaviors. Examples of this are an increase in stress hormones, weight gain, or higher levels of cholesterol circulating in the blood.[72] It is wise to be mindful of this, for we can choose to transform what we hand down to our children and descendants.

Victor Frankl, who experienced the horrors of a German concentration camp, was able to survive by living one day at a time and having the determination and desire to share his experiences with the world when he was released.

---

[71] Pietro Invernizzi et al., "Female Predominance and X Chromosome Defects in Autoimmune Diseases," *Journal of Autoimmunity* 33, no. 1 (August 1, 2009): 12–16.

[72] Nagy A. Youssef et al., "The Effects of Trauma, with or without PTSD, on the Transgenerational DNA Methylation Alterations in Human Offsprings," *Brain Sciences* 8, no. 5 (May 2018): 83.

"Everything can be taken from a man but one thing: the last of the human freedoms—to choose one's attitude in any given set of circumstances, to choose one's own way."

– Victor Frankl[73]

The meaning we give to our lives, the will to continually change and meet each encounter with open engagement, opens the door to the regenerative source of our creation. Change is always possible in the soils of our bodies and in the natural world when we welcome and acknowledge the diversity of all that is living; to remember the important roles of the insects and tiny creatures as well as the more obvious and lovable giants such as the elephant. As we discover our wider relationship to the world and our connectedness to everything, we lessen our grip on fear and are able to live with greater acceptance and harmony.

Recognizing Your Own Song

The Himba tribe of Namibia have a beautiful and unique way to connect their unborn child to its identity and 'sense of place' in the world. This helps the growing infant to feel safe and supported. Before the mother becomes pregnant, she will listen and receive from the natural world the song of the child who wants to be born. She will teach the father the song before the birth. Everyone in the village is also taught the song and sings it to the new baby to honor its arrival. Throughout the child's life the song is sung by the community at all festive occasions.

Listen for the melody of your song, you too can hear it within the stillness and the silence of nature. Encourage your body to sing with it.

[73] Victor Frankl, *Man's Search for Meaning* (Boston: Beacon Press, 2004).

CASE STUDY
Thomas' healing reunion with 'home'

"I can't stand up," the teenager said. "My legs will not support me and my bones ache. I am all hot and feel so weak. I can't even get off the bed to get a drink of water." We were conversing by phone.

I asked all the appropriate medical questions to see whether there was an obvious reason for Thomas' symptoms. I could find none. The problem had come on suddenly in the last hour.

"I want to be better quickly as I have my first day of work at my new job on Sunday and it is Friday night now."

"How do you feel now," I asked?

"Fed up that I can't do what I want, and my legs are not responding," he replied. He usually played a lot of football.

"What do you need and where is the remedy outside of your body?"

"In front of my tummy and chest," he replied.

"What do you see when you bring it to you," I asked.

"A tree where I used to live, the leaves are a particular green color." I waited a moment for him to continue. "Now I am in my old house lying in bed looking at the trees, it feels peaceful."

He digested the whole picture. He started to feel new energy entering his body. "My legs are tingling, and I am feeling less hot."

"Do you like what you see and feel," I asked?

"Oh yes, it is like I am seeing the whole neighborhood where I used to play." I left him to dream into the vision now in his body.

I phoned Thomas early the next morning. He said that his legs were much better now, they supported him, his temperature was normal, and he had slept well. Immediately after our phone call the previous night, he had had one bout of sickness. Thomas was able to go to his first day of work as he had wanted, and he enjoyed the new experience.

We make ourselves feel comfortable in our homes on earth. We make sense of the world in our own ways. This gives us peace and joy, a place to create and play in freedom and safety. This is our true remembering. No one person can do this for another.

> *"The ancient rhythms of the earth have insinuated themselves into the rhythms of the human heart. The earth is not outside us; it is within: the clay from where the tree of the body grows."*
>
> – John O'Donohue[74]

[74] John O'Donohue, *Beauty: The Invisible Embrace* (New York: Bantam Books, 2004).

Thoughts to Germinate

- Working with the dark and light phases of the moon helps us harmonize with the magnetic and gravitational cycles of change and the balanced interplay of the moon, sun and planets.
- We have 'mirror cells' in our bodies useful for recognizing healing connections.
- Our bodies are flowing with energy, and the space that surrounds us is full of informational energy
- Our internal compass is a wonderful guide when we align it with the earth and cosmos.
- Our immune system is our internal reflection of our awareness of Self.
- The aloha spirit of equanimity positively influences our health.
- The doorways of metamorphosis are always open. Approach them now.

Part 4

Practicing Concentra

Chapter 8

The Fire Within

Embodying All That We Are

"There is more wisdom in your body than in the deepest philosophy."

– Friedrich Nietzsche

Many of us in the UK rely on our National Health Service (NHS), which I have been proud to be a part of for so many years. This wonderful idea, conceived in 1948, has many benefits and has been through many changes. One area that it has fallen short though, is in dealing with chronic lifestyle issues and long-term illnesses. The NHS does not engender and inspire the idea of self-care and responsibility. This is one of the reasons I have taken pen to paper.

This book is for those who want to feel free from the label of their condition and complaint, and who want to experience life free from continuous medications that numb the body and dull the mind. It is for people who desire a united mind, body, and spirit, for those who are prepared to fully discover and befriend the fire that lies within.

Do we truly know our own bodies and understand what they are trying to tell us? For many of us, the answer is no, and yet deep within our cells and spaces, we have an excellent communication system. If, as children, we were taught how to listen and feel all our body's messages, we would grow up knowing the freedom that comes from understanding what we are sensing and feeling. When we are encouraged to vocalize our experiences, it helps us to be able to release them soon after they arise. All too often we learn to suppress feelings to avoid conflict because we are told only to express ourselves in a certain way or not at all. How many of us have been quieted by others, or have stopped ourselves from being silly when we were having fun? When we do this, we are dampening our amazing imaginations and inbuilt knowledge.

Unfortunately, we tend to believe others rather than trust our own instincts. Every time we discount our inner wisdom, we lose a part of our spirit and, in turn, the gift of communication with ourselves and others. We give up knowing what we know. These seeds are sown and germinate at a very tender age, and so we continue through life half-heartedly, making less and less of an attempt to be ourselves. On the other hand, perhaps we think we know who we are and bullishly push through life missing out on new experiences. When we are given little encouragement and too many rules to follow, the sense of freedom, fun, and creativity suffers.

We unconsciously write life scripts and now is the time to rewrite them consciously.

When we face continual conflicts and are unable to find peace within our minds, the territory we most need to reclaim is our own, that which is within us. In fact, the further afield we search, the more detached we become from ourselves. My experience is that we will only find our truth with the help of the wondrous vehicle we inhabit: our physical being.

The way forward is through integration of the three brains bringing discernment and balance, illuminating our innate wisdom. Previous epochs relied primarily on these forces individually, or in unbalanced combination, rather than in collaboration and integration. These kinds of outdated relationships are no longer sustainable or desirable and inhibit our return to health.

We are all searching for the same things: happiness, peace, love, health, community, and freedom to follow our own path. We tend to look outside ourselves, rather than being present with what is, until we finally realize the pure intangible essences have been here within us and around us all the time. When we dare to communicate with our bodies and to engage with our felt sense of pain, we are able to summon the answers to these questions and find the freedom we are seeking.

Reclaiming Our Inner Voice

Reclaiming our inner voice of knowing will happen when we really intend to take action. Commitment and determination are required. Check in with your body on a regular basis to become aware of yourself in your surroundings and to listen to the messages inside. The rewards will be more than worth it, because caring for your body means not only caring for yourself, but for your planet, your friends, and your families. The wisdom and courage that will come when you take this responsibility is boundless. The emotional and physical pressures within the body will drop away as we become comfortable with connecting and trusting the more subtle sensations and insights. Balancing the inner sensations with the outer allows harmony to be restored.

This chapter provides various activities for you to practice to help you learn to focus your awareness and listen to your body.

Focusing our Awareness with Exercises

You might have realized by now that I'm not one for following the rules, so with all the exercises I describe in this book, you should feel free to personalize them for yourself. Creativity is the very source of life, and without the possibility of reinvention and novelty we lose heart and die.

As you pay attention and quiet the mind, you will become more aware of what you are experiencing. Examples could include any of the following:

> *"I can suddenly feel my pain, pulsations and spasms, surges of energy and tiredness."* Learn to become aware of changes in sensation and feelings in your physical body.
>
> *"I am suddenly feeling confused."* Learn to become aware of changes to your mental state, such as inner chatter, cluttered and incongruent thoughts, paranoia, or apathy.
>
> *"I am overwhelmed and sad."* Learn to become aware of your emotions, such as the extremes of feelings and all of those in between: anger and love, fear and excitement.
>
> *"I am drifting off into dreams and sleep."* Learn to become aware of how you divert your attention and lose focus.
>
> Learn to become aware of your responses to these changes. Do you resist, withdraw, retreat, push forwards or become blank and numb? What is your default mode, the one you habitually choose? Do you choose different responses for different situations? Changing state is healthy and normal, it is our ability to navigate and master these changes without suffering that is beneficial.

Exercise A - Examining the Breath

First, it is essential to learn to breathe and to truly feel our bodies. The exchange of information as you breathe in and out is important for centering and calming your physiology. Breathing is the key to the bodily states of being energized and of being relaxed. Awareness of the breath requires focus and a constant state of easiness. This allows us to be more powerfully present within ourselves, and it is within this experience of presence that we can work with any obstacles in our minds that may limit or hinder the depth and breadth of any exchange.

As you continue to watch the breath, imagine every cell in your body breathing in all directions, not just your lungs. I have never forgotten seeing a monk seal breathing as it lay sleeping on a black sand beach in Hawai'i. What fascinated me was that the whole of its body was engaged in the process of breathing. During inspiration of the breath, I saw the body ripple from the tail to the head and whiskers and back down again. This is how a baby breathes especially during those initial precious moments after birth.

If you breathe and find a part of our body feels lifeless, painful and disengaged, you can focus on that part and bring it back to life and vitality. The heat generated with every breath is the start of your fire of illumination, so draw it in and up and out into every space.

Let's begin.

Find a quiet place to sit, stand, or lie down, either inside or outdoors in nature. You might find it easier to concentrate with your eyes closed initially, or you can do this with your eyes open, softly gazing.

I love to stand in meditation, outside if possible. For me, experiencing the alignment of my body with my feet firmly on the ground and breathing in fresh air is such a good place to start. Swaying and feeling the air supporting helps me to settle into myself. In contrast, sitting still without first becoming aware of where I am unsettles me. Find the position that best suits you for connecting fully with the earth below.

Do what feels good for you.

- As you stand, or sit, feel your surroundings: the quality of the air, the temperature, the space around you.
- Observe how tense or relaxed you are and yet how supported you are by the ground, chair and air around you.
- Notice how your clothes feel against your skin.
- Listen and feel the movement of your breath inside and out. Observe the energy flowing down and up in the body. Are you breathing only through one part, or is all of you breathing? Are the inhale and the exhale of equal length?
- Feel gratitude for your amazing body that continually supports you in the world.

If I am thinking too much, engaged in my thoughts, the exchange of air brings my energy from my head into my body and the weight into my feet. If I feel heavy and lethargic, the breath helps me to feel lighter, raising my energy ready for the exercise meditation. If I feel overwhelmed and my pulse is racing, I will breathe from my belly to reduce my overwhelm and sense of loss of control.

Observe where you are and watch for the place of ease and balance to arise.

Exercise B - Uniting the body

Now that you are comfortable with Exercise A, we can move on to uniting the body using our breath.

Set an intention for the time you want to invest in the exercise. I find using a stopwatch helps.

Find that inner space of silence and stillness and begin to breathe paying attention to the rate. It will gradually slow down as you settle into the exercise. Slow all systems in your body with your intention.

You may decide to set a certain rhythm for the breath. Exhale for the count of four, pause for four, and inhale for the count of four breaths, repeating for five minutes. With practice, you may decide to extend the exhale to 15 counts. Hold the intention for your body to release into this pattern. No force is required, only the time to faithfully observe.

You may become aware of both the ribcage and lungs moving up and down, forwards and back and in and out, movement in all directions. Experience the pressure difference between the space in your lungs with the space outside of you.

See if you can merge the inner and outer awareness, as if the outline that your ribs create disappears. The space is you and you are the space. After a time, observe the changes in your breath and body.

Imagine an infinity sign (a figure eight) centered from your heart, passing through your lungs to your head and to the sky above, then back down, passing through your heart, down to your pelvis and feet and earth, and finally back to the heart. It is a wonderful reminder of our connection to here and there with every breath.

Appreciate and be grateful for the awareness and energy exchange between the breaths you are now conscious of:

- Give thanks to the universe for highlighting those areas that feel refreshed and alive.
- Give thanks to the universe for highlighting those areas that do not yet experience this.
- Give thanks to the universe for this divine connection of grace between you.

Ask yourself and find one word to answer these questions:

- How does my mind feel?
- How does my heart feel?
- How does my abdomen feel?
- How does my whole body feel?
- How does the outside world feel/look/sound ?

When you have completed the exercise and asked yourself how you feel, talk to your body. It may have highlighted an area for you to explore.

Consider:

- Why am I now drawn to that specific part of my body?
- How does it feel when I touch it? Do you want to feel it with your fingers, or avoid it?
- You may decide just to take a quick look initially if this is unfamiliar territory, or if you sense unease or fear.

How detached do I feel from it? You may have the feeling that one of your limbs is missing, or that you can't feel your feet on the floor, or maybe you want to avoid feeling it completely.

- Enjoy touching and exploring all areas of your body. Your experience may become more pleasurable.

When you start to talk more with your body and desire to know more, your sessions will last longer. Your abilities to develop this inquiry will deepen, as this is a natural communication skill we all have. Continue to ask questions, becoming more intimate and exploring more avenues into and with yourself.

Remember how good it feels getting to know someone for the first time, as if falling in love.

Exercise C - Deepening Into the Intimacy of Feeling

Once you're familiar with observing your body communicating with you, any feelings that you may have pushed away, suppressed or ignored will start to arise.

Begin to delve into the different sensations such as numbness, pain, or odd feelings of which you have become aware. Stay present with them. Are other parts of your body talking? Maybe they tingle, ache, or feel tight? Perhaps you feel a headache or a sense of heaviness? Or maybe you have a feeling of mild panic, nausea, yawning, burping or a sore throat?

Observe and do not judge or attach any particular significance to the experience. Surrender to simply experiencing. This process you have consciously set in motion continues even when you are not actively observing it.

When you make time for a session, hold no expectation for your experience. Your body will communicate a new awareness, though it may be very subtle. It is important to remember that if you believe there to be a physical problem, it may not be entirely true. It is simply something, an awareness of pain that has become highlighted. For example, the awareness of pain in your abdomen may not always mean there is something physically wrong with it. Of course, you experience the pain, but when tested, scanned, and examined, the cause may not be found. Pain is your body's way of communicating disharmony. Undiagnosed pain is extremely common. I prefer to relate to these areas as uncomfortable, ill at ease, or disturbed.

The body knows the perfect way to re-establish flow and harmony, and it will bring to your attention the part to be dealt with first. Following the order and structure presented to you is the best way to release the pain experience. Within each sensory experience, there may also be an emotion, or emotions. This could range from happiness, sadness, anger, rage, resentment, guilt, confusion, pleasure, or something else entirely. You may feel relaxed, overwhelmed, lost, or even have a sense of nothingness. Release any judgements; simply feel and experience what is presented. We are blessed as humans to experience such a wide variety of polarised emotions as fear and excitement, love and hate. To deny any is to deny a part of feeling alive. As we experience the emotions, they change rapidly as we continue to acknowledge them.

Talking with Ease

Once you trust your body as a true friend, one you can confide in and really listen to, the conversation will become easier. When we look curiously at emerging situations and engage with the silent space, the body relaxes. There is an ally, a companion always on hand to ask advice from, helping with difficulties and uncertainties; together you become a secure loving partnership. Sometimes we do not know the question that will help us. Trust that by simply asking the body, it will always illuminate the doorway which is both the entrance and the answer to the question.

Over time, your own knowing will start to emerge out of the awareness you perceive in your body.

Make the time to structure your day using this internal focus, whether before work, on the way to the office, or even sitting on the toilet! Learn to go within whilst at the computer, waiting for an appointment, and standing in a queue. During working hours, our emotions can be suppressed, we tend to focus outwards and we become numb to our own needs. This enables us to cope with long hours, fatigue, and daily challenges. Tiredness and stress become the daily theme and we all know that this mode of operating is not sustainable without something giving way.

Relieving Stress in our Bodies

Stress is a state of being when we are not aware of our true selves.

Much has been written about the word 'stress.' It's like the word 'pain;' It cannot be seen or measured accurately. It is unique for everyone and manifests in numerous ways in our lives. Stress, or we could use the word 'pressure,' stems from the gap between what is present and our acceptance of it.

We already know that every cell and structure in our bodies is a barometer, dynamically changing, communicating with the next cell to facilitate good health (See Chapter 3). When we experience an emotional or physical event that challenges our inner perceptions and beliefs, or in extreme, our feeling of our hold on life, we respond in one of three ways. We can freeze and go blank; run or fight and become overly excited; or we can disassociate from our bodies and enter another state of consciousness. This can last for a few seconds or much longer.

In these conditions, the body is in what is called sympathetic dominance. This response registers in the amygdala in the brain and is normally only fully used if we perceive our life is being threatened.

In wild animals, this stress response is only present for up to 90 seconds after the danger has passed. The protective system then switches off and the body rebalances and may discharge the excessive energy as shaking. However, as humans we often remain in that heightened sympathetic state. Our body is so concerned with protecting us from our imagined attacker, that our immune system, digestive system and hormone systems react as if we are always under threat and are unable to perform their normal functions. Over time, this new operating system we have unconsciously created begins to feel normal to us and we lose touch with our natural way of being. We forget the way back to balance in response to our daily non-life-threatening stresses. The amygdala becomes continually activated, which requires energy and thought, leaving little space for the awareness of anything else. We have less capacity for insights, resourcefulness, and resilience to situations we encounter. For as long as the body remains in a stressed protective state, it cannot heal fully, and has less resistance to illness and disease. We can lose our ability to be playful and creative, and our loving juices dry up.

The good news is that as we begin to watch the feeling, sensation, and emotion of 'stresses,' they dissipate, no longer the driving forces of our behavior. The stress hormones that were constantly produced by the repeating alarms in the systems gradually diminish and the body releases healing hormones such as oxytocin, dopamine, nitric oxide, and endorphins. The body's own self-healing processes operate when it is at one with the 'stress.' 'Stressing' is initially useful, as it reconnects us to ourselves once again, urging us to pay more attention and navigate back to our center. It may take an accident, a significant life event, or just an awareness that the balance is off in our lives for us to choose to do this.

When we give ourselves the space to heal our energy body and all parts of ourselves, the amygdala, nervous system, and all of the physiology involved will return to their innate natural resonance, our natural harmonic state. We start to feel alive again, resonating more fully with our DNA. Our physical tissues follow suit.

Exercise D: Relieving our stress

This exercise helps us to focus, stay present, receive inspiration, and experience clarity of mind.

Spend at least 15 minutes for this exercise to alleviate your feeling of stress or pressure.

Choose an activity and make it the focus for truly staying alert and present. This could be for example, gardening, walking, cooking, or talking with another. Choose to engage with the activity with increased focus for two weeks.

As you undertake the activity,

- Perform it more slowly than usual.
- Watch your actions.
- Feel every movement your body makes during the activity.
- Feel the effect of your actions as your body moves through the environment.
- Be observant, noticing any sounds, smells, and tastes.
- Observe creation unfolding.
- Every two minutes return to the stillness and silence within your body.

Let's take cooking as an example of an activity you might choose.

Be clear with the intention of your creation. As you pick up the knife, feel its heaviness, the texture of the handle, notice the sound it makes as it cuts through the food, the solidity of the ingredients, the change in the state and colour of the food, the smells released.

Consider the experience of your body standing or sitting preparing the food, the joints and muscles you use, the actions performed for each task, the slowing down of your senses, heart, and body.

Notice if any thoughts draw your focus away, your response to the different stages of the task.

The more details you notice, the greater focus you will achieve by the end of the 15-minute activity. How do you now feel about this experience? How are you in relationship with your new creation?

These are a few ideas to help you to experience more awareness in simple, everyday tasks. It is a way to begin to experience our whole lives as a meditation. Journaling the awareness may help you to embed the expansion in awareness you have witnessed.

Coming Home to Our Bodies

As we continue to work through the process of understanding the communications from our body, our awareness in everyday life increases, and we may find ourselves naturally wanting to make different life choices. We might feel the desire to meditate, make time to walk in nature, or seek the advice of a nutritionist or dietician to help us to find better food choices. We could find ourselves joining a walking group, volunteering, or choosing new ways to engage with our body. There are many ways we can support our journey of expanded awareness, such as flower essences, homeopathy, acupuncture, essential oils, emotional freedom technique, yoga, qigong, tai chi, forest bathing, prayers, chanting and tantric practices.

There is no doubt that it's sensible for us to look after our body and enjoy it in the best way we can. All these practices are helping us to find our inner selves again, to BE US! To know what we know without fear, shame, or becoming overwhelmed.

The answer is present inside of us now.

To own our body completely, inhabit our territory and know every nook and cranny, every blemish, every wrinkle, or separated part, is to truly accept ourselves. And once we realize that our body is the vehicle to knowing ourselves, the interface of reconnection, we can take care of it while at the same time letting our physicality go. As we fuel it with respect, love, gratitude, and daily nurturing, all of life responds. By realizing that we are not 'this' or 'that' in particular, but that we are all of it and none of it, the anger, doubts, frustrations, and confusion drop away, revealing the love that we are.

"What you seek is seeking you."

– Rumi

Thoughts to Germinate

- The body as a barometer registers differences as stress, which is a message for us to find answers, recalibrate, and balance ourselves.
- The body is a faithful friend who guides us to our deepest knowing.
- Exercise A: Familiarizing with your own breath.
- Exercise B: Using the breath to center and unite the body.
- Exercise C: Observing and dialoguing with your feelings and sensations.
- Exercise D: Remaining present to relieve stress with everyday tasks.

Chapter 9

The Elemental Wisdom of Nature

"To know thyself is to know nature."

– Hippocrates

"There is no energy in matter other than that received by the environment."

– Nikola Tesla

Over the years, these two quotes have regularly popped into my mind. What were they pointing me to and reminding me of? They have certainly guided my writing and own direction of healing and it is this wisdom that I would like to share with you now.

My Golden Moments of Enchantment

I remember the beauty and warmth of the sun, shining through the trees, dappling the water as I splashed my little net into the stream hoping to find something new to examine. The cold water felt so good flowing around and past my shins as I gripped the slippery stones with my toes. The yellow light glistened on the water and back into my body sending sparkles everywhere. I observed the water as it glided towards me, the stream's flowing nature, navigating the rocks in its path, coursing both to the left and right before merging and approaching the next bend further downstream. Those English summer days spent outside were so very magical and gave me many meaningful connections to such simple joys.

I did not realize that these elements of nature were so integral to my well-being until I spent time working in hospitals, in darkened, airless basements. These 'health revelations' ensured that I actively pursued spaces that were full of light and surrounded by clean air and natural warmth, important nourishing energy for my body. For 25 years, a clinic on the edge of the English Channel ticked all the boxes.

My Favorite Re-memberings

"If you are in bad mood good for a walk.
If you are still in a mood, go for another walk."

– Hippocrates

We do not need extraordinary intelligence to know the 'feel-good' factor that our natural world brings to us. The pleasures of a walk in the countryside and taking in an expansive untouched view, the freshness of the sea air, or the beauty of a single flower held perfectly still by the wind, are joys anyone can appreciate.

I remember those much-loved picnics eaten outside on the beach, the gusts of wind playing havoc with the sand, giving a grainy crunch to every bite. They will always be more memorable and enjoyable than one sandwich consumed inside a car, bereft of the aliveness and vitality of the elements.

I remember the longed-for first cold sip of water after a day's hike under the sun, temporarily forgetting how good water tasted.

I have listened to rain gently dropping onto leaves and then bouncing off. As I watched their downward journey of song, my troubles seemed to wash away.

I have delighted at the spider's fine web remaining true, beautiful and connected, even during a fierce storm.

I meditate with a flower and become the wisdom and beauty that it holds.

"Medicine is the restoration of discordant elements; sickness is the discord of the elements infused into the living body."

– Leonardo Da Vinci

These personal memories are wonderful examples of the healing powers that nature brings us. Over the past 20 years there has been a growing interest in incorporating nature as a prescribed remedy for conditions such as heart disease, high blood pressure, depression, and anxiety. Measurable markers of stress, such as raised levels of cortisol in the blood drop whilst walking in forests, and patients comment that they also feel a greater sense of wellbeing. In the 1800s, walking and breathing in the air of pine forests was prescribed as a treatment for tuberculosis. Sea bathing, breathing in the negative ions produced by the ocean or submerging oneself in the expanse of blue, has been a remedy for generations. Perhaps one day we will once again see more of this type of 'medicine' replacing or being given alongside drugs.[75]

Patients in hospitals recover quicker and need less painkilling medication if they have a view of leafy trees in natural light. Even a picture of nature on a hospital wall has great benefits.[76] More and more research shows that spending time in green spaces has huge health benefits. A study of 20,000 people revealed that if a minimum of two hours per week is spent in nature, individuals were more likely to report good health and psychological wellbeing. Another study highlighted the presence of lower crime rates and greater community cohesion with exposure to green spaces.[77]

---

[75] Christoffer van Tulleken et al., "Open Water Swimming as a Treatment for Major Depressive Disorder," *BMJ Case Reports* 2018 (August 21, 2018): bcr-2018-225007, https://doi.org/10.1136/bcr-2018-225007.

[76] Deborah Franklin, "How Hospital Gardens Help Patients Heal," *Scientific American* 306, no. 3 (2012).

[77] Jim Robbins, "Ecopsychology: How Immersion in Nature Benefits Your Health," *Yale Environment* 360, (2020).

Forest bathing, or shinrin yoku as the Japanese name it, has been used for many years in numerous countries as a therapy to improve health. One of the benefits is that whilst among the trees our blood becomes flooded with immune cells called "natural killer" cells. These immune cells help protect us from infection and tumors. We literally 'absorb and inhale' the essence of nature into every part of our being. Our pockets are filled with gladness. We have been blessed with more than just five senses with which we can use to deepen our connection to the natural world. Michel Cohen has identified 54 distinct senses.[78]

"Climb the mountains and get their good tidings, nature's peace will flow into you as the sunshine into the trees. The winds will blow their freshness into you, and the storms their energy, while cares will drop off like autumn leaves."

– John Muir[79]

The natural world not only heals us; it is essential for sustaining health. The subjective sense of loneliness is known to have a detrimental effect on our physical and mental health and shortens our lives; some say this is more dangerous than obesity or smoking 15 cigarettes a day. We are wired to live as a social species and healthy interactions are helpful nervous system modulators. However, with the cultural shifts in living arrangements and the speed at which we run our lives, spending quality time with others often falls by the wayside. If we engage with nature when we are alone, moving with the changing clouds, cycles, and seasons, the experience of isolation recedes, and balance, harmony, and direction return to our lives. The sense of separation dissipates and all relationships benefit.

---

[78] Michael J Cohen, *Reconnecting with Nature; Finding Wellness through Restoring Your Bond with the Earth* (Lanham, MD: Rowman and Littlefield, 2007).

[79] John Muir, *The Mountains of California* (San Francisco: Sierra Club Books, 1989).

"Those who contemplate the beauty of the earth find reserves of strength that will endure as long as life lasts."

– Rachel Carson[80]

We can transform our physical bodies with the elements of nature. There are some plants that give us nutrition and then there are those that help us to detoxify, strengthen, and regain health. Many Western drugs are derived from the chemical components found in plants. Though beneficial, these separate elements are mixed in sterile petri dishes and have not synthesized and evolved together through the energies of the cosmos and soil. Which has greater benefit for your body?

Nature Teachings from Bon Shamanism

In 2013 I bought the book Healing with Form, Energy, and Light[81] by Tenzin Wangyal Rinpoche. I read it once and then left it alone on my bookshelf. I was reintroduced to it again a few years later by my friend Anna. The book's essence lies in the teaching of Tibetan Bon Shamanism, one of the oldest lineages predating Buddhism in Tibet. It resonated with me immediately and over the years I have always gained much wisdom from the text.

In the Bon tradition, our entire being is understood to be the balance of the subtle energies and qualities of the five elements of nature. In addition to fire, air, earth, and water, they see space as a fifth element. By befriending nature and becoming intimately familiar with it through the senses, informational patterns appear for the renewal of our physical body and our lives. New structured connections between the inside and out begin to form.

---

[80] Rachel Carson, *The Sense of Wonder* (New York: HarperCollins, 1965).

[81] Tenzin Wangyal Rinpoche, *Healing with Form, Energy and Light* (Boulder, CO: Shambhala Publications, 2002).

Dzogchen Buddhist teachings say that by communing with nature, we are awakened to that which was believed lost and yet is already inside us. The loving cooperation of our natural world nourishes and supports our bodies, minds, and souls.

Tenzin Wangal Rinpoche gives to us the "Three Pearls of Wisdom:" Stillness, Silence, and Spaciousness. These qualities in our bodies are essential to fully experience nature and to become one with the elements. By cultivating stillness of the body, infinite awareness through silence and spaciousness and the warmth of an open heart, we connect to our center of profound healing. This 'inner refuge' is our natural sacred state of peace, aliveness, and wholeness.

"Natural forces within us are the true healers of disease."

– Hippocrates

The Five Elements of Nature

I would like to introduce you to the five elements of water, fire, air, earth and space. As we deepen our connection to them, we start to experience our inherent nature of calmness and the ability to transform pain, 'dis-ease,' and disturbances in our lives. As we become one with each element, we return home to ourselves.

Each of the elements is an aspect of the primordial energy, the energy from which everything is created. The creative patterns are forever present all around us. Perhaps you know it as the 'chi' field. As we engage with every new subtle awareness, we feel that sense of being alive, connected to a never-ending supply of nourishment. Nature never, ever says it has given enough. It is present, reliable, abundant, constant, and available 24 hours a day, and is always changing. It is one of our greatest teachers. Continuing to feel grateful for all we have received and continue to receive from the earth, is an important start in beginning our reconnection.

"Whatever is flexible and loving will tend to grow, whatever is rigid and blocked will wither and die."

– Lao-Tzu

Many a time I have felt overwhelmed by my personal interpretation of something. By going outside and exhaling and then taking in the balanced patterns of the elements, I find I am able to settle my disturbed internal physiology. The elemental energies move through me, and feeling their vitality, I remember how to dance once again with myself with a new awareness of inner freedom. From here it is easier to see new perceptions to the problem and drop my opinion. The natural resonances of nature can lead us back to our own harmony.

"When all the strings of my life be tuned, my Master, then at every touch of thine will come out the music of love."

– Rabindranath Tagor[82]

What does this quote from the Indian poet Tagore refer to? Our senses help us to integrate the sound waves of displacement, the feeling waves of misalignment in the body, the visual waves of distortion, the thinking waves of belief and judgement and the pressure waves of distress. As we become more familiar with this fine tuning, the skin, surfaces, and all boundaries disappear and direct contact to all of creation becomes possible. It is as if we become one with the cosmos, fully belonging as part of the creation story.

Make it a desire to become aware of your daily communication with nature

[82] Rabindranath Tagore, *Stray Birds* (London: Macmillan Co., 1916).

The integrative practices I suggest in the book become easier with repetition. New awareness emerges as you spend more time 'being nature'. Sit down, invite yourself to know yourself better through the essence of each element. Decide to spend at least 20 minutes with each to deepen your friendship with them. Some people prefer to return to the same place in nature each day to establish this connection.

Feel guided by my words and yet, more importantly, always led by your own heart's song of yearning. You are the only one who truly knows the sound of the harmonies of the elements in you.

Elemental Metaphors in Everyday Speech

Listen to yourself and to others using the elements in everyday speak. Things like:

- I feel a bit spaced out.
- I can't breathe, it is all too much.
- I feel all over the place.
- I feel a bit weepy today.
- I am boiling up inside.
- I feel pent up, ready to explode.
- I am all at sea.

Which elements do you think are out of balance in these statements? Every element has many dynamic patterns of energy and we are each born with a mix of these subtleties. We are always more comfortable in the familiar pattern we hold now. Giving structure and balance and space to all elemental harmonies creates a completely new rhythm and tune. Adapting an old rhythm or running with spontaneous jamming sessions are sometimes necessary for us to hear a melodic resonance again.

"Happiness is not a matter of intensity but of balance order rhythm and harmony"

– Thomas Merton

The Element of Water

We are made of more than 75 percent water, and the mineral composition of our plasma fluid resembles that of seawater. The sea connects all lands and countries joining every part of our earth. It gives shape to islands. More than 75 percent of the earth is covered by water. It is the essential element, giving shape to life both inside and outside of our bodies.

Water is a mediator, the connector to our emotions, the medium in which to release and re-establish flow. It is able to both hold information and transmit it too. Water dissolves what is solid into a solution. Given the right conditions, water creates ice crystals, beautiful and unique in design. Cleansing and healing with water brings forth both physical and spiritual regeneration.

Water is shaped to the container it fills, dispelling the air in the process. It can appear churned up and muddy but if left to settle, clarity returns. We can use the water element to access the information held in our blood from our ancestral heritage and change our future.

Forms of Water to Sit With and Meditate On

Whether it be a waterfall, cold stream, babbling brook, a raindrop, or the ocean, the refreshing and revitalizing quality of moving water always nourishes and gives space to new thoughts and emotions. Have you ever watched the water flow around a rock in its path? New currents and ripples create a bypass to the obstacle in the way. Have you observed the currents of the sea flowing in opposite directions, or giant waves crashing against the cliffs which over time erode the rocks into different forms, perhaps revealing the fossils hidden inside?

Whether the water is in the form of a droplet of morning dew, or as finer particles seen rising from the earth's warmth in the early morning mist, this movement and transformation sustains life and connection. Let us not forget the underground streams, those puddles and deep mountain springs that seep through into the crust of the earth. We cannot be without water.

Too Little or Too Much Water

When we lack the fluid properties of the element of water in our spiritual lives, we can become stuck with situations and projects. Emotions can get the better of us and nothing flows—we dry up and all pleasure is lost to us. We can lose our caring, peaceful, and loving nature.

When we hold excess water, stagnancy can exist. An inland lake without a continual fresh source of water will at some point become choked and overcome with decomposition. We drift, deciding not to take charge of our own direction. If the water is too deep or cloudy it can appear a challenge to see through it.

Nourishing Ourselves With Water

I love those moments of letting go. A refreshing shower running over and through the body washing away any troubles; a warm bath penetrating the tiredness of a long day; the comfort and peace of being held by the ocean and the sensual rhythmic brushing of the currents against the skin; or the power of the waves tossing you in the surf. Tasting water drawn directly from a deep well, or sipped by cupped hands from a mountain stream, still has the vitality and clarity from its original source. Oh, such simple pleasures.

My Water Experiences

On a post-Christmas walk in the rain across the Kentish Hills, I stopped to look up the hill and saw two streams of water running towards me on either side of the lane. The uneven surface and low light made the undulating water feel as if it was moving towards me at a fast pace. I turned to look down the hill. The same streams appeared as if moving towards me again. I turned again quickly. In that instant I could feel that I was actually standing in the middle of the converging water with it rushing through me up and down the hill. A moment of being in the flow!

On another occasion we had hiked down to the Queen's bath on Kaua'i. It was a rough, windy day. There were big waves breaking into the pool, which had been created by the surrounding lava rocks. Many people were watching, and a few were taking the opportunity to have fun in the pool, navigating the force of the waters. I wanted to join in too, so I jumped in from the rocks. After a large wave broke into the pool, someone shouted at me to swim to the front of the pool as fast as I could or the current would pull me backwards onto the rocks behind. I am not a particularly strong swimmer, so I felt the anxiety rising in my body. We waited. The first swell came in, water pouring into the pool. A second wave followed immediately from a different direction. As I felt myself under the great force of the water, I decided not to fight with it. I trusted and allowed the energy of the two waves to hold me. To my delight when I surfaced, I found I was in the same place, not needing to swim anywhere for my safety.

Despite the intensity of what you perceive rushing towards you, as you become one with the energy, there is peace.

When I recall these sensations, I can now feel these calm stable places inside.

In recent years, the Kogi peoples have come down from their mountain home in Colombia to help us all to remember that water is the source of everything. If its flow is stopped at the source, or blocked at the outlet, the process of recycling cannot begin again. The life-giving cycle of water is halted. All waters merge and unite with each other, whether it is the stream that runs into the river finally meeting the sea or the rain falling from the sky which turns into mist and blends with the rising vapors from the earth. These water sources of life sustain the golden threads of relationships which continually unite us all.[83]

---

[83] "Aluna," movie website, accessed September 2, 2021, http://www.alunathemovie.com.

Meditation for Building Your Relationship with the Element of Water

Before you begin the meditation, thank the element of water: *"We thank you water for the life-giving essence of your spirit and for the cleansing and clarity that you bring. Let us remember how to maintain our loving and flowing connection now."*

Begin the meditation with the breathing exercise as described on page 168, Exercise A

After cycling the breath up and down in your body, imagine it moves through your heart. Your whole body is breathing from your heart and receiving the breath back. It pulses to your rhythm with the earth. As the heart and the infinite space connect, rest your mind in this calm expanse. Give yourself this time and space to fully prepare in the present.

Choose a situation in which you feel uncomfortable or uneasy. Experience it through as many of your senses as possible, immersing yourself deeply within the experience whilst using the cycled breath.

Ask yourself "What type of water connection will help me move with my chosen emotion and state of being?"

Feel the healing water permeate your being, seep into every cell and the supporting and protective waters around the heart. Stay with this flow and awareness for as long as possible. Absorb the energies of this connection fully.

You may also choose a memorable and pleasurable time with a water experience and deepen your connection this way.

The Element of Fire

Fire is the element of regeneration and action. The 'fire in our bellies' helps with digestion and transformation of energy into matter. Fire focuses us, directs our attention and passions. Fire is purpose and clarity of vision and connects us to the sun and solar system. It brings joy and drive and willpower, guiding us to light up lives.

A focused direction of awareness generates this spark of firelight.

Forms of Fire to Sit With and Meditate On

The sun, at dawn, midday and sunset, a volcano, a campfire, a raging forest fire, the radiating heat rising from the earth; all supply us with fire energy. The smoke of a fire is a sign of transformation before the ashes appear. The sun and the twinkling of a multitude of stars forever give us strength. Your own inner fire, whether gently burning or flaming furiously, provides informational and transforming energy for you and others. The balance of a steady, bright, gentle, and strong flame will continue to nourish many.

Too Little or Too Much Fire

When our fire is not truly alight, inspiration, joy and vitality are absent. We become cut off from our life force and from pleasure. Indecision and inaction are present. Creativity and the power of regeneration seem far away.

With an excess of the fire element, agitation, intolerance, explosive emotions, and instability can arise. It may be difficult to sit still, focus, and concentrate. Swinging emotions may result in impulsive decisions and the heat of frustration may fuel interactions and decisions that are later regretted.

The Building of My Inner Fire

When stoking a fire, I start with the right foundations: smaller wood at the bottom and then a triangular shape with larger logs on top. The use of paper or dried leaves will help to spread the fire as well as keeping it alight. Once alight and consistent flames are seen, more wood is applied, and the burning logs are moved to expose more of their surface to the heat. I noticed I was always reticent to move the logs and expose more surface, believing that the ignited fire would continue without further help. I learnt that more attention to keep the structure open would enhance its aliveness. After starting many fires and seeing them peter out, I learnt the importance of watching, blowing air, and adjusting the wood at the right time.

I love a log fire that warms you from the inside out, penetrating deep into your bones, its benefit continues long after the embers die down. The next morning it only takes one spark to rekindle the fire as the ashes are still aglow from the day before.

Charge your inner fire with energy and light that you may always know your blissful dance with the flame and sparks within.

Meditation for Building Your Relationship with the Element Fire

Before you begin the meditation, thank the element of fire:

"We thank you the element of fire for the warmth, strength and focus of your presence. We accept change as the encouragement to reach beyond, for all of our creations."

Begin the meditation with the breathing exercise as described on page 168, Exercise A

After cycling the breath up and down in your body imagine it moves through your heart. Your whole body is breathing from your heart and receiving the breath back. It pulses to your rhythm with the earth. As the heart and the infinite space connect, rest your mind in this calm expanse. Give yourself this time and space to fully prepare in the present.

Choose a recurring thought, decision, or situation for which you desire change, perhaps where you have lost your creativity and joy.

Or breathe the warming fire of regeneration into a part of your body for physical healing.

Or watch the leaves as they move catching the light rays of the sun.

What type of fire and warmth will help me transform my chosen state of being?

Feel the fire permeate your being, seep into every cell, deeper into the blood and bones and stay with this nourishment and awareness for as long as possible. Watch and experience the transformation of the physical body in the heat and the rising smoke.

The Element of Air

Air connects everything. It is the element we share with all living organisms. We create unity within ourselves by breathing with our whole being. Air diffuses into water, it holds magnetite, and it is impossible to keep a fire alive without it. We cannot see this element, only the effect it has, such as when the vibration of a voice communicates its message to us. It is air that creates the atmosphere in which we live, both internally and externally transmitting the cacophony of vibrations we are exposed to. Air creates the movement of the leaves rustling in the trees and the drifting of the clouds high in the skies. The element of air brings to our lives the attributes of curiosity, learning, and flexibility. Each one of our inspirations and exhalations of breath is an appreciation of life and creation.

The Vitality of a Breath of Fresh Air

Breathing life into seemingly dead, stuck, and painful parts of our bodies creates healing, similar to when we call for new perspectives to solve problem situations. With a fresh inspiration, inventive ideas spring to mind, sparking our imagination.

We can nourish ourselves in the presence of wind: walking briskly to the top of a hill, breathing deeply and feeling the strength of the wind at the higher elevation; watching kites or sailing boats capture the wind in their sails; befriend the wind rustling the leaves, listening to the music they make together. Imagine and feel yourself shooting an arrow through the air. Aim, hold onto nothing and at the point of the exhale, release it, listening to the sound of the arrow travelling through the air to its final destination.

Too Much or Too Little Air

When we do not use our full capacity of breath and stop the air from reaching all of our being, worries can overwhelm us and we remain in our small minds, excessively thinking. We are unable to move the energy fully around our bodies. We lose clear vision, going around in circles with the same rigid thought, our sense of playfulness missing. This airless space becomes 'too close' for comfort, and we sometimes prefer to stay where we are than seek a change in situation.

With too much air, we lose our center and become scattered and fragmented, an airhead, indecisive and pulled by the directions of the winds we meet. We lose our inner gravity. We have difficulty staying in contact with the comfort within ourselves and our sense of contentment becomes elusive.

Meditation for Your Growing Relationship with the Element of Air

Before you begin the meditation, thank the element of air:

"We thank you, the wind for supporting our being, for the breath of air that renews us daily. Together we give honor and gratitude for the shared breath of all our creations."

Begin the meditation with the breathing exercise as described on page 168.

After cycling the breath up and down in your body, imagine it moves through your heart. Your whole body is breathing from your heart and receiving the breath back. It pulses to your rhythm with the earth. As the heart and the infinite space connect, rest your mind in this calm expanse. Give yourself this time and space to fully prepare in the present.

Choose a thought or situation where you feel stuck and lack the flexibility of movement and change. Desire to bring in more playfulness and lightness. This may be a good time to remember a joke and belly laugh!

Or remember a time when the wind was your friend, blowing new perspectives and ideas into your space.

Or remember the time of a 'shared breath,' the belonging and nurturing qualities of relationship with another, whether it be a person, plant, place, or animal.

Feel the qualities of the wind element bringing the newness of inner freedom into every space of your mind and body.

The Element of Earth

We have come to rely on Mother Earth and her sustaining and solid foundation, for she continues to give us so much. As we become more intimate with the fertile womb of earth and dialogue with the animals, insects, trees, plants, and rocks, we forge new relationships, healing our bodies. The appreciation and reverence generated when at one with nature, heals us both at our core.

The land speaks; we must learn how to listen. The soil, once so full of life sustaining nutrients and insects is becoming depleted. Over-mining for precious metals continues at an alarming rate. We are called to account. Many species of animals, plants and seeds are being lost forever. Indigenous peoples are losing their homes and ability to survive from the land. It is from these wise elders we must learn how to care for the earth and share in her abundance whilst preserving her beauty; for the rocks are our bones and the life-giving rivers are our blood. Walk gently on the earth for every footstep creates a vibration. I remember taking a walk in the Blue Mountains of Australia with a young Aboriginal man. At the very start of the day, he requested that we leave no trace of our footprints, quietly experiencing, allowing for the continuum of the wild creative spirit of nature.

Lack and Excess of Earth's Grounding

With a lack of earth's stability in our lives, we can feel anxious and ungrounded, with no base of support. We lose trust in all that is around us. In the extreme, we let go of all responsibility. We lose the ability to receive the minerals that the earth offers us, and we become ill.

With an excess of earth, we can become lazy and stubborn, fixed in our behavior and thoughts, even if they are not serving us. Problems may appear insurmountable, and we can become depressed and disillusioned.

Nourishment from the Earth Element

Let our feet be open to give and receive gratitude for all that is provided as we share our earth home. Walk barefoot on the earth, lie on the grass, put your hands into the soil, allowing your connection and reverence to grow. Watch the worms and other microorganisms working together, cooperating to sustain life and generate fertile soil. Trace the roots of a tree into the ground, feel the strength of a big mountain or a stretch of gently rolling hills.

Plant yourself in nourishing soil, a seed with wisdom, in tune with the seasons, and with the hum of the earth. Germinate, thrive, and flourish, producing new seeds to be scattered. Gain insights from nature and the elementals working together, creating harmony and beauty for us all. Learning how to communicate with plants is a wonderful way to grow your connection and physical health.

The Transformative Earth Time of Dusk

This is such a beautiful period of the day, the twilight zone neither dark nor light. As the day ends, the night falls. Witness the pause after the sun has set where the world is so still and peaceful and before new energy lightens the horizon joining to the sky. It is a wonderful space of healing and rejuvenation. The trees and plants begin to enter the transition phase. The light absorbed from the sun is released as fluorescence from the leaves as they give back to the universe. They are whispering and dialoguing with the sky as the darkness descends, their radiant energy creating their own response to the day.

What do we do on a daily basis to gratefully give back all that we have received?

Flower Teachings

For me, flowers are one of the ultimate expressions of the magic of alchemy; the product of the elements weaving together on earth. Their beauty and individuality are seen in the radiating pattern of the petals—curved, pointed, or feathery—and the vibrancy of color symbolizes a wealth of graceful presence. Some flowers are so delicate and gentle; others single, strong, and bold, each intricately arranged and defined. We love and accept all designs in the flowers, their beauty evident for us all to see.

"The fairest thing in nature, a flower still has its roots in earth and manure."

– D. H. Lawrence

Flowers turn their heads towards the sun, their food source. This is called heliotropism, which enables their photochemical cells to receive maximum exposure to the light. They draw to them helpers that will continue their legacy: the bees to pollinate and birds to spread their seeds far and wide. Perfect teamwork! Flowers will increase the sweetness of their nectar to attract the worker bees who then work tirelessly for the good of the hive and the queen bee.

When we know what another needs, do we offer without a thought?

The receptacle in the flower's center is aptly named the torus, the same word given to the pattern of the field that emanates from black holes, the heart, and the mitochondria.

Did you know that sunflowers give off blue light? Yet invisible to our eyes, we are aware of the joy and wellness we feel when experiencing a multitude of them within our own field of vision.

Did you also know that plants release sound? The study of this is called 'plant bioacoustics.' Stressed plants release a greater number of sounds thought to be caused by the cavitation of air bubbles in the transporting tissues, the xylem, as water is drawn into the stem. In areas of drought there is more resistance and noise in the xylem as water is less available.[84]

The yield from crops can be altered by broadcasting waves of certain frequencies.[85] Even their gene expression and metabolism can be changed with sound frequencies.

"There is mana in the flower that has blossomed slowly."

– Hawaiian proverb

Like a flower, your inner sovereignty and beauty arises with patience, time, and the union of the vital forces of the elements within this mana flow, you too will be empowered and radiate this presence to others.

---

[84] I. Khait et al., "Plants Emit Informative Airborne Sounds under Stress," December 2, 2019, https://doi.org/10.1101/507590.

[85] Reda HE Hassanien et al., "Advances in Effects of Sound Waves on Plants," *Journal of Integrative Agriculture* 13, no. 2 (February 1, 2014): 335–48, https://doi.org/10.1016/S2095-3119(13)60492-X.

Meditation for Building Your Relationship with the Element of Earth

Before you begin the meditation, thank the element of earth:

"We thank you for your continuing support and benevolence, your forgiving compassion and abundant nature. We bless this living connection. We remember now how to lovingly cherish one another's growth."

Begin the meditation with the breathing exercise as described on page 168.

After cycling the breath up and down in your body, imagine it moves through your heart. Your whole body is breathing from your heart and receiving the breath back. It pulses to your rhythm with the earth. As the heart and the infinite space connect, rest your mind in this calm expanse. Give yourself this time and space to fully prepare.

Feel a situation in which you want greater support and find that deeper connection within yourself by meditating on or visiting a familiar place in nature that gives you strength.

Feel the nourishing warming support of earth permeate your whole physical being, supporting and holding you with firm, rich, loving gentleness.

On another occasion choose a flower or tree to engage with and find the essence of that healing connection. Flowers can bring different energies to us. For example, the honeysuckle can bring movement and joy into the present as you release past memories. The birch tree brings cleansing, shedding of the old, and vision of the new path.

"Your way of knowing is a private herb garden.
Enclose it with a hedge of meditation,
and self-discipline, and helpfulness to others.

Then everything you've done before
will be brought as a sacrifice
to the mother goddess.

And each day, as you eat the herbs,
your garden grows more bare and empty.
Beautifully full of juice they come from the mother
causing many birth pains.
Again and again, they wait at her door to enter."

– Lalla [86]

[86] *Naked Song: Lalla*, Trans. Coleman Bark (Athens, GA: Maypop Books 1992)

Space

All elements arise from space and dissolve into it. The element of space manifests as emptiness and from this darkness everything arises. When we are centred and connected, we can accommodate what naturally arises in 'our space,' no requirement to resist or become caught up in it. When rooted in ourselves, the one who is experiencing, We, Us, You, I, we are present with wisdom and understanding.

Space can be perceived in many forms, such as the space within matter; the space of the sky, cosmos, and black holes; the space between the stars; our own personal space around our bodies; and the spaces in which we live. Our communities and families represent a wider picture of space.

Too Little and Too Much Space

With too much space we become 'spacey' and 'spaced-out', disconnected from the physical world. We lack presence and focused awareness and wait for things to happen. Inactivity may follow. With too little space, we become dominated by what arises. Small problems become big when we confine, pinpoint, label and rationalize problems. If we give greater space to the disharmony, we find acceptance. For example, if we only look at the stars in the sky we are missing the space!

Nourishment from the Space Element

By gazing at the sky or an expansive view we can connect with the space element. Listening to the song of a bird and becoming that feathered body gliding with the currents is a good way to deepen our relationship with space. Australian Aboriginal elders are known to meditate on the sky to prepare for the last part of their life journey before death.

A rainbow is an example of space, water, air, fire, and light together. We can never truly find its wholeness or grasp it, and yet it will always be a delightful mystery. Fire and air have no physicality to them, yet they are visible. Fairy stories and legends say that revelations and blessings greet us at the end of the rainbow.

When looking and feeling the pain in your body, be open to the spaciousness of the sky. Allow it to enter your body and heart and remain in the space long enough to return the 'pain sensation' into the space of its origin.

Meditation for Expanding Your Relationship with the Element of Space

Before you begin the meditation, thank the element of space:

"We thank the container of space, the boundary-less continuum that is present with everything. We welcome this vastness that helps us to remember our presence."

Begin the meditation with the breathing exercise as described on page 168, exercise A.

After cycling the breath up and down in your body, imagine it moves through your heart. Your whole body is breathing from your heart and receiving the breath back. It pulses to your rhythm with the earth. As the heart and the infinite space connect, rest your mind in this calm expanse. Give yourself this time and space to fully prepare.

Connect to the blue sky and to the vastness of the heavens above. Stay with the openness of the space outside and inside as you remain sitting comfortably on the earth. Feel the nourishment of this eternal essence, a space of rejuvenation.

Or meditate with a rainbow: dive into the colors, climb it, discover the ends and the blessing in its creation.

Merging with the Elements

As we become more familiar with communicating once again with each element and with all that nature holds, we develop greater sensitivities, experiencing more subtle energies. We begin to recognize and befriend these forces. The essence of each element brings us back to the qualities of our authentic self—openness, awareness, and warmth.

We experience the subtle patterns of each elemental encounter; the sound of water as the rain bounces off the ground, a plant, or the sea; the heat of the sun shining on the earth; or the fire thundering out of the ground in a volcanic eruption followed by black smoke snaking into the sky. Be sure to also listen to your internal flame that sparks others to shine ever brighter.

Allow time to be with each element, strengthening your centre, creating new patterns of awareness, and releasing the old. Continuing to meditate and breath with plants and trees enables us to deepen our experience with their healing essences.

Breathing through the quality of stress or pressure whilst being able to remain calm is a quality that nature teaches us. On earth we feel wind pressure, water pressure, pressure from hot and cold, and also from the earth. Different places feel unique. We feel pressure or tension from situations, other people, and can be overwhelmed by what we see, feel, and hear.

Tension is what forms us and we are held in varying forms of tension, postures, shapes, and states. A certain amount of tension is necessary or we would collapse into a heap on the floor. Too much tension and our muscles complain. Navigating from this point of tension helps us to move and release unhelpful states of being. As I have become more aware of the changing pressure as my body registers the external world this navigation is easier.

Thoughts to Germinate

- The subtle essences of the elements will guide us to our essential qualities of openness, awareness and warmth.
- The living world cooperates using natural laws. Experiencing and living this wisdom helps us to navigate our lives.
- Direct experience and integration of the elements transforms unwanted physical, mental and emotional manifestations.
- Nature is a bridge between our physical and spiritual being.
- Our health benefits in many ways by communicating with nature every day.

The sun is reflected in both the salty waves of the sea
and in the clear surface of a mountain lake.

Seeing things with physical eyes is not enough,
You must experience the inner significance of the thing seen.

– Swami Nityananda[87]

[87] Chetanananda, *Sky of the Heart*, 134: 196.

Chapter 10

The Concentra Process

"We but mirror the world. All the tendencies present in the outer world are to be found in the world of our body. If we could change ourselves, the tendencies in the world would also change. As man changes his own nature, so does the attitude of the world change towards him."

– Mahatma Gandhi

Now that we have integrated the breathing practices and the exercises for deepening awareness with the body, we can learn how to 'Concentra'.

Many situations respond well to the Concentra process, including those shown below, but the list is by no means finite, so do experiment for yourself.

- Any representation of pain in the body.
- Manifestations of illness and disease.
- Behaviors you want to change.
- Repetitive loops of unhelpful and judgmental thoughts.
- Beliefs that repeat patterns of disharmony in your life.
- Emotional swings that cloud the clarity you wish to experience.
- Shocks and traumatic events stored in the body.

Concentra will also help with:

- Deepening communication with your subtle senses and innate gifts.
- Establishing and maintaining healthy, loving, and nurturing relationships.
- Re-centering and experiencing life through an opening of the heart space.

Here I describe the full process, which you will be able to shorten once you are familiar with the steps.

Helpful Tips Before You Begin

- If you have a balance issue, please do the exercise sitting down, as it can cause a shift in your center of gravity.
- You may feel a little confused, so avoid driving for ten minutes, or until clarity returns.
- You may suddenly experience tiredness as the body integrates the new vibrations.
- You may experience shaking and trembling as the muscles relax into the healing phase.
- Please drink more water than usual following the session to facilitate the changes.

Preparation

It is worth taking the take time to settle into your inner stillness, silence, and quiet spaciousness. This will help you experience the wisdom guiding you to activate the changes you intend to create. Give yourself time to undertake Concentra. The full process can take anything from five to 30 minutes.

Creating Inner Stillness

Start to gently breathe from the lower abdomen, facilitating the breath to move up to your chest. Slow the length of each inhale and exhale. Feel your feet resting on the ground and the space around them. Sit comfortably and as straight as you can, with or without support. Become aware of relaxing the end of your spine. To connect the energy from above and below breathe into your feet and up into your head connecting to the sky above. Rub your hands together to connect the left and right.

You may choose to do this with your eyes open or shut. Imagine the breath moving up and down from the feet to above the head in a wave or pulse. Follow this natural pattern of movement within you.

After cycling the breath up and down in your body, imagine and encourage the breath through your heart. Your whole body is breathing from your heart and receiving the breath back, pulsing with the rhythm. As the heart and the infinite space connect, rest your mind in this calm expanse. Give yourself this time and space to fully prepare.

Identify Your Intention for the Session

What do you want Concentra to help you connect with? What is your intention for the session? For example:

- Release the pain of your knee.
- Release and understand the solution for your abdominal pain.
- Help change anxiety, fear, or guilt.
- Exchange anger and overwhelm for a calm and grounded feeling.
- Help with decisions for the changes you want to make in your life.

- Help to stop smoking, or to eat more mindfully.
- Gain inspiration for the new plan you are putting together.
- Improve your relationship with something or someone.
- Bring focused awareness and clarity to a meeting, exam, or important event to ensure the best outcome.

Identifying the Area or Areas to Work with in Your Body

When you have created your inner stillness, silence, and spaciousness though the breathing exercise described, ask your body to show you where your chosen intention is located in your body, if you have not already been made aware of it. Watch for and tune into any sensation, pain, numbness, or emotion in that place that your consciousness reveals to you.

Witness the location in your body as deeply as you can and scan for other places that may be connected to it. Do they feel impenetrable or far away? If so, illuminate them further with the breath. If you need to increase your awareness, speed up the energy in the area by rubbing your hand over it, spinning it in all directions.

Draw to your awareness all the emotions, feelings, or sensations that arise with that intention. Do not push away what you perceive as 'bad' emotions, such as anger, fear, and jealousy. We are here to experience everything. Witness and explore the colors, smells, or tastes and sounds that may surface before they release. You may hear a word or phrase. You are now in the process of exchanging experiences with the vastness of space around you.

Acknowledge what arises and release any story around the problem. Send your logical analytical brain far away. You are working with energy, your sensory intuition, awareness, compassion, and inner guidance.

Watch your inner experience and allow everything that arises. Marvel at how your body changes so quickly given the space to move. You may feel tingling, weightlessness, light, confusion, or a change in temperature in some or all parts of your body. You may want to move and wriggle parts of your body. Notice the posture you are holding, perhaps a tight hand, a furrowed brow, or holding of the breath. On the other hand, you may find nothing, simply a void.

The greatest healing will take place when you surrender and rest deeply in the awareness. When you feel your body has revealed all parts connected with the pain or issue, it is time to transform it further.

The Space Around You

If it has not happened already, find a space outside of yourself that connects with this bodily experience. The answer to the pattern is already present in the universal field of all possibilities and as yet has not been fully realized in you.

Look to all of the 360-degree space around you. Once you sense the solution, the vector of the matching energy, draw it towards you, breathing it in. It may also appear as a shape, a circle, sphere, or triangle, or it may be a spark, color, or sound. Feel the energy in the areas of your body that are wanting this gift of healing. It may feel like a vibrating rhythmic bubble flexibly moving to meet the similar likeness in you. This moving energy may be familiar, or it might be unknown.

In this quantum space, you may experience yourself as a little child again, you may be among the stars and planets, or in a green field. You may see an animal. You may experience nothing, or confusion, or a sense of relaxation, joy, and spaciousness. Your inner child may want to be loved, held, and appreciated. Often you are healing wounds and memories from the past and future. Everything is possible. Watch and feel the physical changes in your body at the same time.

Choose whether you like this new experience or not. It is your choice to accept it and breathe it in, or to exhale it away from your own personal space. Revisit your intention or physical area of pain and notice the changes. The sharp pain may now be an ache, or it may have totally disappeared.

Expand the new feelings with your breath into all cells, fully connecting to your heart, head, and pelvic areas. The body will do this automatically, but sometimes it may need some extra guiding help. Rest in this experience.

These new connections will also resonate out into the space around you—above and below, in front and behind, left and right. Breathe them out as far as you can for the healing benefit of everyone. This 360-degree rebalance is essential for manifesting the solution inside and out.

Each time you repeat the process of Concentra, a new experience awaits you. You are facilitating profound changes by witnessing and opening to the emerging awareness. You are exploring yourself as consciousness, expanding out into space and touching on greater possibilities. By letting go of control and trusting the experience, your innate wisdom can choose from the field of infinite possibilities, rather than from limited experiences and imagination. Try to refrain from overthinking. Your spacious heart, the inner eye, is guiding your vision.

If you feel vulnerable or uncertain, hold yourself gently with love and tenderness. By engaging with your newfound direction of energy, you open to new creative solutions and new beliefs from within—a growing sphere of love, mutuality, gratitude, and wisdom.

If you encounter resistance or stickiness and the energy exchange has stopped, it may be helpful to use the questions below to continue the release:

- *What will I feel like after this is transformed now?*
- *How will I see my life changed?*
- *What do I need right now to proceed—for example, reassurance, love, safety?*
- *How does it support me to stay as I am?*

Continue to nurture and hold yourself, watching the supporting love you are both giving and receiving. Drop more deeply into the stillness and silence. Call on the elements of nature to help you with this transformation. Which element or elements can help you? For example, it could be water, perhaps gentle falling rain, or the great ocean waves cleansing you? (See Chapter 9 for more about the wisdom of nature.)

If you notice an attachment to a feeling that blocks further progress, use the Hawaiian family prayer of forgiveness Ho'oponopono to release it (Chapter 6, page 137). These moments of forgiveness can be pivotal in this process of transformational exchange.

Spontaneous Physical Changes Felt and Seen

As you are transitioning through the process, generating new energy states, you will feel a variety of symptoms, comforting signposts that the solution is emerging. Examples of this could be itching of the skin, goose bumps, burping, yawning, a new smell or taste in the mouth, sudden heat or cold in the body, a cool breeze against your skin. You may become more aware of the still air around you. It may feel settled, quiet, and peaceful. Some may experience shaking of the body as the nervous system and muscles let go of knots and tightness. Initially anger may arise before other emotions. In my practice, I witnessed an Indian client immediately starting to smell coriander, which reminding him of his mother; another smelt mango shower gel; and another patient could taste and smell sponge cake.

New Physical Experiences

As you continue to watch, breathe, and acknowledge the changes, continue the process:

- Your breath may be lighter and more expansive in your body, and it may become easier to breath.
- You may have an awareness of an inner smile, knowing all is well, feeling a joyful release, safety, or a sense of moving forward. Outwardly there may be a change in facial expressions, such as a softening of the brow, skin perfusion (flushing), smiling, and youthful appeareance.
- Your voice may change, expressing with a greater range of tones, or originating from a deeper place within your body.
- You may be aware of a part of your body that previously felt separate but now feels heavier, or calmer, after relaxation of muscles that were previously tight.
- Your bones may hurt.
- The physical movement that was previously painful is easier. Examples might be: lifting your arm up, turning your head, squatting, or balancing on one leg.
- Your focus of intention has shifted and become more aligned within you.

Nothing has changed but your awareness.

Deepening the Friendship with Your Body

Walk on the earth now with new purpose and alignment by exploring the movement that was a problem, repeating it five times to store it in your neuro-muscular system as the new program. Remember to continue to do this five times a day for a week to facilitate muscle memory and for the nervous system to fully integrate the new pattern.

- Touch the relaxed muscles, feeling the new sensation of softness.
- Observe the feeling of improved posture—the neck and spine naturally more erect, the body remembering the innate knowledge of its true alignment.
- Notice that walking has become more rhythmical, steadier, and requires less effort.
- See the world more clearly, alive with greater color.
- Listen to the greater silence and freedom inside and out.

Congratulations: you have exchanged perceptions and expanded your awareness.

Give thanks in the following dedication: *"Thank you for this healing. I offer these new healing connections to all beings so that they too may be free from similar suffering."*

If you prefer not to speak out loud, allow yourself to relax and let go into this expansive space of silence inside and out. This is as profound as any spoken words.

Learnings from Concentra

As awareness of the new space becomes more familiar, new connections form within and without. The revelations and learnings may come in the form of words, or a felt sense of change, and you will appreciate and understand them both. You may choose to say, "I am aligning fully with all my new understanding now."

Ongoing Changes

The healing connections continue as you align with the new awareness. You may witness all manner of mysterious or familiar sensations seemingly unconnected to the original pain. This could be tiredness and aching as a result of the energy moving through, dispersing accumulated toxins. You might experience increased discomfort or odd reminders of pain in the areas you brought the healing to. It may seem like a crazy time with emotions rising and falling rapidly. Use your breath and inner flame to blow away any that are persistent.

Further Miracles – Synchronicities Abound!

As we passionately embrace life with no expectations or boundaries, the unexpected happens.

Having taken the time to Concentra, you may find greater benefits or experiences than your original intention.

You might:

- Join that yoga or dance class, or start swimming again, not because you know you should, but because you want to. Perhaps you will enjoy exercise for the first time.
- Change your relationship with food/smoking/addictions, not solely through determination and willpower, but because the new relationship with your physical and spiritual body requests it. It will require less effort.
- Apply with confidence for that new course or job you have been putting off, no longer fearful of outcomes.
- Decide to undertake something you would never have dreamt of before.
- Start to lose weight naturally and discover your perfect way of eating.

- Find that the phone call you dreaded is now a different experience.
- Sleep longer, feeling more refreshed on waking.
- Feel more comfortable and alive enjoying being in your body.
- Find your physical digestion and digestion of life is easier.
- Feel more optimistic and trusting of the future.
- Centre yourself with greater ease through the ups and downs of life.
- Become more aware of how others around you are feeling.
- Make wiser, more informed decisions in your life.
- See the gift in all situations.
- See other ways to be of service to others.
- Find that those perceived difficulties in relationships at home and work become easier, finding solutions more easily where there are differences.
- Find job opportunities and life experiences synchronously appear.
- Resolve a previous problem such as selling a house or finding the money for a project.
- Start to notice the numerous omens and synchronicities that are guiding you.

As you truly experience yourself in harmony and flow, there is no stopping the creativity that follows. Engage with and nurture it. Continue to radiate joy, love, and gratitude for all the support and blessings you are receiving. This is the most valuable energy source for the heart.

Using Concentra with Another Person

Some people may find it helpful to use Concentra with another person who will act as an observer. The observer is present to hold an open, questioning space and guide the individual back if they lose direction or become stuck or analyze too much. They can give positive feedback on changes they see, boosting confidence in the other. When there is more than one person, the accumulative effect of the reconnection is far greater, for everyone is both a giver and receiver for each other.

Sometimes using a codeword or sound to encapsulate your intention for the session can be useful when working with another person. Choose the word when you identify the area of pain you wish to work with. The codewords or sound will remove the emotional charge from the issue as well as represent the real meaning for you at a deeper unconscious level. The word could be an actual representation such as 'blocked' or 'horrible' or a randomly chosen word such as 'apple.' It may work for you to make up a sound or word like 'Blahzoh.' You could also use a posture to represent it, a screwed-up face for example, or a clenched fist.

As you start working with another person, feel yourself present in your whole body using the initial preparation stages as before. Set an intent to hold a loving space for the energy to flow and continue to breathe. Ask for the guiding wisdom and support of all higher loving forces to reveal what is needed. Use the steps as written for individual Concentra.

CASE STUDY
Alex and his left shoulder pain

Alex's intention was to heal his shoulder and make more supportive loving connections in his life. He was a body therapist and liked to cycle and swim and had been unable to work for three months, having sustained a tear in a tendon in his shoulder. This had been identified through an MRI scan. He had received one steroid injection and was taking strong painkillers daily.

Alex had suffered the same problem on the right shoulder a few years earlier. Progress was slow and he was impatient to return to work. He was keen to take the time to really get to the bottom of the problem, rather than temporarily fix it with another steroid injection, which had not worked the first time.

During my first session with Alex, he was unable to lift his arm to the side more than 40 degrees without pain. When he performed this movement quickly, he felt an acute sharp pain. He was also unable to reach his hand very far behind his back. After he had showed me what was possible for him with his shoulder, we started to talk. I asked him to go inside his body and feel everything that became available for him to witness.

"I have been really fed up during the last ten days, in a bad place. I have been eating a lot of carbohydrates and sugar, uncontrollably. I recognised this and yesterday I decided to stop, as I know it is causing me more pain and not helping my tendon recover."

He patted his stomach.

"What color is the area you are patting," I asked?

"Grey, kind of foggy."

"What have you been eating?"

"Jellybeans, lots of them. All different kinds."

"What do they remind you of?" I asked.

"When I was a kid, our family used to eat lots of sugary things for breakfast—and jellybeans."

We fell into silence. "It makes me think of my dad."

"Family connections," I said. "A meal shared together?"

"Well, I don't remember much of that," Alex said. He thought for a moment and started to wriggle his painful left shoulder and arm. "My dad was a good guy. He is dead now. I remember when he got me into his old school, even though I did not have high enough grades."

"Did you make the most of it?" I asked.

"No, I only lasted one term. I did not choose to go there. I see now that my father must have really wanted it for me and helped get me in." He shook his arm and looked into the distance. "I never really said thank you or appreciated his efforts on my behalf."

"Was he cross that you left his old school so quickly?"

"No," and I saw him experience the surprise.

"I see a deep blue/green colour that I have never seen before," he said. "In front of my shoulder."

A gentle breeze was felt by us both. Then the air became still, and Alex became aware of the red bird singing in the trees.

"Experience the pattern, rhythm and pulse in your heart and body," I suggested. We sat in silence.

"I can feel my father here now, supporting me. It feels so good." Alex took the time to stay resting in this space of awareness and feeling the energy in his heart. I asked him to speak with his father if he wanted to and to say whatever he felt.

Alex felt a connection to the area he had patted in his abdomen that was previously gray in color. I waited as he spoke with his father. He sat up straighter. "It is red now," he said, referring to his abdomen, and he started to test the movement in his shoulder. "It feels different and more connected."

He continued: "I know that I should be eating more alkaline things to reduce the inflammation. What do you think would help my tendon?"

"What does your red tummy say?"

"Wow," Alex replied. "I can see juicy red strawberries

and pomegranate seeds. I enjoy eating them both. I love those little red and purple seeds. They seem like jewels to me."

"Did you know that pomegranate is good for your heart and your circulation and connecting with your pelvis?" I said.

We talked about how he could ask and sense what his body wanted to eat, the benefits of lemon and water in the morning, fresh ingredients, and taking the time to prepare what he needed for himself.

"My shoulder still hurts," Alex said. "And it is down the back of my arm now, as well as a point on the front of my shoulder." He pointed to the areas.

"Any change is good, for it means your body is responding to your dialogue with it. Do you like the new support you are feeling?"

Alex reflected back to his father. "Yes, I feel much happier."

"Bring those feelings and energy that you like into the areas that hurt and to every area of your body and tell me of your experience," I requested.

Alex recalled the blue/green color and saw it coming into his body. He saw his cells as red and inflamed. He watched a little more and then said: "No they are not inflamed. I can see them becoming healthier, transparent with a clear light. I see an octopus with its eight legs holding the cells together."

He looked relieved. I asked him to look deeper, to the outside of the bone where the tendon was attached. I started to massage the point that was sore, and his pain began to diminish.

"I see a black area underneath the clearer cells. It doesn't feel good. I want it to go."

"With love, ask the blackness to leave, breathing it out and thank it for making itself known to you," I said. Alex did as requested. We both breathed out and relaxed into the opening.

"I see the cells turning into water, flowing and massaging the area, like the sea with crystals in it. It feels really good. I like that."

"Perfect," I replied.

He reflected for a while on what he had experienced. "The red that was my inflammation was not like a burning flame from a destructive fire. It was more like the radiance of the sun. I must remember that."

Alex lifted his arm and it felt lighter and he could tell he was using it differently. "The pain is much less now, and I can move my arm behind my back almost as far as the other one. I am more aware of my whole body."

I asked him to continue to breathe the flowing liquid into his heart and radiate into all areas from his head to feet and beyond. I felt that Alex had reached a balanced point for the healing to continue without further input for the moment.

"Well done. See what you can achieve for yourself with help from everything around you?"

Alex nodded and recalled the points he wanted to remember and use from the session. "I feel better about my shoulder healing now on its own and finding a partner to share my life with."

I gave him some exercises as homework to use specific muscles to embed the new relationship he had with his shoulder.

We gave thanks for the help with the healing that we had both experienced, breathing this deep into the body, grounding into the earth and out into the cosmos.

Themes arising from Alex's experience with Concentra

- The expression of disharmony in Alex's relationship with food: he was using jellybeans to draw a closer connection with his father and with himself. Alex became more conscious of listening to his body for the foods that would help him feel and experience the harmony he wanted (red fruit).
- Change is good even if it feels that the area of the pain is getting bigger.
- The use of colors: the gray fog in the abdomen which changed to red; Alex's changing perception of red, first as inflammation, then as the color for his healing; the red of the tendon changed to clear and transparent; the black area, deeper on the tendon which he chose to let it go; and the awareness of the outside colour of deep blue/green used by Alex internally to make a beneficial change.
- Muscle relaxation: when Alex felt a deeper and more supportive connection with his father, the shoulder area became more pliable and the pain on the tendon itself reduced.
- The importance of experiencing new sensations in the heart, abdomen, and area of pain which Alex felt as connecting with his whole body.
- The spontaneous assistance from elements of nature: Alex naturally brought the fire, air, earth, and water into the session along with sound and light. He tasted, touched, saw, and heard his way into the space where healing could take place.
- The spontaneous visualization of animals. Receiving the 'medicine' of the octopus and continuing to dialogue with this manifestation will continue the healing gifts that Alex has received. Further dreaming with octopus 'medicine' may also help.

What People Say After Their Experience of Concentra

"It catalyzes you into change."
— John

"That's bonkers! You mean my pain was nothing more than that?"
— Maria

"I am not sure what happened.
It feels like I have just woken up."
— Eva

"I am just so happy I can start over."
— Mary

"Feels like I have had a biblical experience."
— Claire

"I feel bigger with more space."
— Tim

"I see the new golden wiring in my body."
— Emma

"The blue light is shining above me."
— John

Thoughts to Germinate

- Feel the joy of experiencing your own body's ability to change.
- Practice flowing with the greater wholeness in you.
- Rejoice when you ask for help, knowing your prayer has already been answered.
- Communicating intimately with the 'pain' opens you to the healing connections you desire.
- As we take action for change, we heal our bodies by releasing the energy of the held state.

Full Circle

"If you are always trying to be normal you will never know how amazing you can be."

– Maya Angelou

We can all find ourselves overwhelmed at various times in our lives, feeling incomplete and at a crossroads. In my travels and exploration of the wisdom of different cultures, I found a way to be with this deep, restless longing and to release the reins that I sensed were restraining me in my life. My quest led me to realize the presence of this healing power within me and this understanding became the basis for the simple process of Concentra.

Pain is a moving consciousness rather than a static state, and when we choose to fully investigate our experiences with it, we find connections to memories or past traumas, and to future regeneration and healing. This takes place on an individual level as well as on generational planes affecting our descendants and society as a whole. In this act of remembering, our pain changes and our health flows again. Uniting the heart, mind, and speech through the physical body is the foundation to authentic self-expression. Aligning our body's compass with the grids of the cosmos and the earth allows the healing energy to freely flow, connecting us directly with the universal heart. From this point of integration our sense of wholeness returns, and we can step forward into the world with confidence. Our spiritual relationship to this mystery of life regenerates, inspires, and sustains us.

I am continually amazed by the many physical transformations I have witnessed that spontaneously occur when we are guided by these invisible informational structures accessible to us in the quantum space. Ancient indigenous wisdom continues to provide wonderful teachings for us in the modern world. We have the ability to enter the wakeful dream state and release pain, as well as give and receive gifts from past and future generations. This commitment to our own healing benefits others as well as ourselves. As we choose to live as nature's presence, we will fully breathe once again, sharing the breath with others as we did at the beginning of time—as liberated, cosmic citizens.

One of my favorite books as a child was Ferdinand the Bull. I always wondered why I wanted to read it again and again and why I have kept such a torn and tattered manuscript. Ferdinand did not behave as a traditional bull; the matadors enticed him to fight, yet he preferred to sit under the tree smelling flowers. Are you willing to give yourself the permission to be the true individual that you are? I have looked within and am committed to the Ferdinand within me. The healing language of nature and flowers will forever be at the center of my own heart.

"Once you trust yourself then you will know how to live."

– Johann Wolfgang von Goethe

Acknowledgments

Special thanks and appreciation

Thank you to the people who have inspired my work and taught me so much over the last 30 years.

To all my patients who provided me with years of practise and Ah-ha moments, those patients who had faith that together we could find solutions to their health and challenging life situations. Thank you for sharing your stories.

I thank Dr Philip Bull for putting his faith in new clinical practises.

I thank the inspiring teachers I have had on my journey: Bob Elvey, David Butler, Pete O'Sullivan, David Stone, Richard Flook, and Charles Matthews.

To my dear supportive healing friends, Lindsay Thompson, Christine Dupre, Lyn Rich, Anna Bonas, and Suzette Kale. To Claire Reid who ventured on this journey with me and who is the most wonderful friend and ally.

A big thank you to Nic Evans, Loring Robbins and Arnie Kotler for their numerous editing and restructuring sessions. Thank you for your patience and encouragement. Blessings and thanks to Su Swan and Francisca de Zwager for their skill and gentle nudges for walking me through the design and maze of self publishing.

To the Hawaiian peoples and islands, I thank you so much for sharing your gifts of aloha, timeless wisdom, and traditions. I honor the land, the ocean, the animals, and all of nature and I pray that we give space now for a more loving cocreation.

And finally, to my family who have supported me: my daughter Emilia, one of the catalysts for writing this book; my son Silas, who has pushed me to go deeper and relinquish more; and my loving parents, who showed me how to be resilient and curious with all that I meet.

Hawaiian Petroglyphs

Hawaiian Petroglyphs or Ki'i Pōhaku are carvings etched in the lava rocks by the Hawaiians many centuries ago. Some are obvious depictions of forms we recognize, others are symbols for which we may not know the intended meaning. It is said that places with mana, cosmic power, are chosen for the rock carvings.
The following descriptions are my interpretations.

Part 1: Circles

In Hawaiian mythology circles represent creation and a life without beginning or ending. A larger circle with a smaller solid circle in the middle may represent the birth of a baby into the family and two circles another sibling. It is a symbol of the piko or belly button from where we are connected to the Mother. This symbol represents the Great Spirit and Mystery and from where all new life arises.

Part 2: Turtle

There are five species of honu on the Big Island of Hawai'i, the greenback turtle being the most common. She links the people, the land and the sea, and is thought of as a worthy navigator helping all who honour her to find purpose and direction in their lives. She represents endurance, stability and longevity and is recognized for her wisdom. It is said that the markings on the shell represent the 13 new moons that appear in the sky every year.

Part 3: Canoe

Without the canoe and excellent navigation skills the Hawaiians would not have discovered their islands. In mythology the canoe is the vessel that carries us around the milky way as we come to know ourselves and the skies above. To be recognized as a master canoe builder was a great honor and privilege. The craftsman would visit a forest and ask the trees which one had been chosen to become the next canoe. Wood from the Koa tree was the most widely used. Traditional canoe races are still held around the islands celebrating this sacred vessel.

Part 4: Man and Woman

The carvings of people begun as stick figures and later the man was represented by a triangular form. Often they were depicted holding a paddle, spear or perhaps a gourd used for hula ceremonies. The woman's shape appears more rounded like a sphere.

Thoughts to Germinate: Taro Blossoms

The taro plant in Hawai'i is held sacred. It is the state plant, recognized as one of their ancestors. The stem represents the ha, the breath and the shoots the ohana and family. In this way the individual is represented and the environmental, social, and cultural values that are important to the Hawaiian peoples. Kalo is its Hawaiian name and it is a one of the 'canoe crops' first bought with them for their survival. All parts of the plant are eaten. Poi is made from the root which is alkalising to the body and said to be good for bone structure.

Further Reading and Listening

Nature Connections

Lori Bailey Cunningham, *The Mandala Book. Patterns of the Universe* (New York: Sterling Publishing, 2020)

Peter H. Fraser, *Energy and Information in Nature: A Collection of Papers on the NES Health Theory of the Human Body-Field* (Poole, UK: Choice Point Communications, 2012)

Bear Heart with Molly Larkin, *The Wind Is My Mother: The Life and Teachings of a Native American Shaman* (New York: Berkley Books, 1996)

Janna Levin, *Black Hole Blues and Other Songs from Outer Space* (New York: Random House Audio, 2016)

Marlo Morgan, *Message from Forever: A Novel of Aboriginal Wisdom* (New York: HarperCollins, 1998)

Daniel Stone, *The Dreamer Who Dreams You* (Winchester, UK: John Hunt/O-Books, 2005)

D.M. Urquidi, *The Popol Vuh: An Astronomy Book par excellence* (Texas: dmu Ink, 2011)

Popular Science

Jill Bolte Taylor, *My Stroke of Insight: A Brain Scientist's Personal Journey* (New York: Penguin Books, 2009)

Bruce Lipton, *The Biology of Belief* (Santa Rosa, CA: Mountain of Love/Elite books 2005)

Pat Masumoto, *The Healing Power of the Hawaiian-Style Belly Laugh* (Makawao, Hawaii: Yes Seminars International, 1995)

Candace Pert, *Molecules of Emotion: The Science Behind Mind-Body Medicine* (New York: Simon & Schuster, 1999)

Lissa Rankin, *Mind Over Medicine: Scientific Proof That You Can Heal Yourself* (Carlsbad, CA: Hay House, rev. ed. 2020)

Esther M. Sternberg, *The Balance Within: The Science Connecting Mind and Emotions* (New York: W. H. Freeman, 2001)

Spirituality

Ferrini, *Love without Conditions* (Parrish, Florida: Heartways Press, 1994)

Carolyn Myss, *Anatomy of the Spirit: The Seven Stages of Power and Healing* (New York: Bantam Books, 1997)

Jetsunma Tenzin Palmo, *Into the Heart of Life* (Boulder, CO: Snow Lion/Shambhala, 2011)

Penney Peirce, *Frequency: The Power of Personal Vibration* (New York: Atria Books/Beyond Words, 2009)

Philippa Anne Rees, *Involution: An Odyssey Reconciling Science to God* (Somerset, UK: CollaborArt Books, 2013)

Lisa Romero, *The Inner Work Path: A Foundation for Meditative Practice in the Light of Anthroposophy* (Hudson, NY: Steiner Books, 2014)

Jean Shinoda Bolen, *The Tao of Psychology, Synchronicity and the Self* (San Francisco: HarperOne, 2004)

Dr Thynn Thynn, *Meditate without Meditating: A Daily Life Mindfulness Practice Manual* (Sebastopol, CA: Sae Taw Win II Dhamma Foundation, 2017)

Nana Veary, *Change We Must: My Spiritual Journey* (Honolulu: Institute of Zen Studies, 1989)

Tenzin Wangyal Rinpoche, *The True Source of Healing: How the Ancient Tibetan Practice of Soul Retrieval Can Transform and Enrich Your Life* (Carlsbad, CA: Hay House, 2015)

David Whyte, *The Three Marriages* (New York: Riverhead Books 2009)

About the Author

Alison has penned the details of her journey from the start of her career as a physiotherapist in the National Health Service in London to the publication of this book. Working with patients and her own physical body led her to appreciate that to truly heal, the mind and spirit must also be at One. This understanding led her to seek out wisdom from indigenous cultures. Recently the islands of Hawai'i called to her, a place to continue her journey and realize her unfolding visions. The subtle whispers of the elements of nature together with the spirit of 'aloha,' the presence of the sacred in all things, continue to be her wonderful teachers.

www.feelhealshare.com

Praise for Daring to Feel

Alison is an outstanding physiotherapist who combines a novel integrated approach to her work with patients, her results over the last 30 years of association have been exemplary. This book is a fascinating read for those involved with holistic pain management.
Dr Philip Bull FRCP, Consultant Rheumatologist

As I was reading this book, it helped me remember a disagreement I had with a good friend about a year before. I realised that bearing a grudge was pointless and that we are all entitled to our own opinions. That evening my long standing shoulder pain had gone and I could move my arm freely and without pain.
Jennie Carter MA, Role of Language in Education

If you found value in the content of this book please share your message with others so it can continue to help more people. One way that you could do this is to leave a review where you bought this book.

Thank you for your help.

Printed in Great Britain
by Amazon

10925230R00140